A RIVER RUNS THROUGH ME

A Book on the Baptism of the Holy Spirit with the Evidence of Speaking in Tongues

W.K. Alsop

WestBow Press
A DIVISION OF THOMAS NELSON
& ZONDERVAN

Copyright © 2014 W.K. Alsop.

All rights reserved. No part of this book may be used or reproduced by any means, graphic, electronic, or mechanical, including photocopying, recording, taping or by any information storage retrieval system without the written permission of the publisher except in the case of brief quotations embodied in critical articles and reviews.

Scripture taken from the New King James Version. Copyright © 1979, 1980, 1982 by Thomas Nelson, Inc. Used by permission. All rights reserved.

WestBow Press books may be ordered through booksellers or by contacting:

WestBow Press
A Division of Thomas Nelson & Zondervan
1663 Liberty Drive
Bloomington, IN 47403
www.westbowpress.com
1 (866) 928-1240

Because of the dynamic nature of the Internet, any web addresses or links contained in this book may have changed since publication and may no longer be valid. The views expressed in this work are solely those of the author and do not necessarily reflect the views of the publisher, and the publisher hereby disclaims any responsibility for them.

Any people depicted in stock imagery provided by Thinkstock are models, and such images are being used for illustrative purposes only. Certain stock imagery © Thinkstock.

ISBN: 978-1-4908-5599-8 (sc)
ISBN: 978-1-4908-5600-1 (hc)
ISBN: 978-1-4908-5598-1 (e)

Library of Congress Control Number: 2014918275

Printed in the United States of America.

WestBow Press rev. date: 10/28/2014

This book is dedicated to the two loves of my life:

To my first wife, Barbara, who walked with me for twenty-seven years. She helped me mature in so many ways with her wisdom and patience. Barbara went home to be with the Lord on Mother's Day, 1997.

To my second wife, Cathy, who has walked with me for the last sixteen years. Cathy has been my encourager, best friend, and faithful partner. She is truly my gift from God.

No man is as blessed as I am with the precious gift of these two women in my life! To Him be the glory!

On the last day, that great day of the feast, Jesus stood and cried out, saying, "If anyone thirsts, let him come to Me and drink. He who believes in Me, as the Scripture has said, out of his heart will flow rivers of living water." But this He spoke concerning the Spirit, whom those believing in Him would receive; for the Holy Spirit was not yet given, because Jesus was not yet glorified.
—John 7:37–39

CONTENTS

Introduction ix

1. Faith and the Spirit Realm 1
2. My Story 11
3. Historical Events before the Day of Pentecost 23
4. What Is Baptism? 39
5. The Day of Pentecost 48
6. To the Ends of the Earth 66
7. The Traditions of Men 89
8. The Benefits Package 107
9. 1 Corinthians 14 124
10. The Modern Day Explosion 151
11. Conclusion 168

INTRODUCTION

On August 21, 2013, the Lord told me to write a book on the baptism with the Holy Spirit with the evidence of speaking in tongues. I normally receive some form of confirmation, and this confirmation came as He began to give me the book outline over the next few days. The purpose is the same as that of all fivefold ministry gifts: to equip the saints for the work of ministry and to bring them into spiritual maturity on different doctrines in the Bible.

The disciples' faith and obedience to the instructions given to them by Jesus would unleash a mighty and powerful tool and would revolutionize Christianity from that day on. Jesus told them that they would be endued with power. They would wear His coat to perform His works. That coat would be placed on them on the day of Pentecost, igniting the last days' movement of the Holy Spirit on the earth, and culminating in the soon return of our Lord Jesus Christ, who will finally establish His kingdom on earth!

My own spiritual walk was dramatically transformed by this gift and promise in April of 1980. I didn't receive it through denominational doctrines; I received it by faith. I received it though I was thoroughly ignorant of the Scriptures concerning it. I had been wholly unaware of any sound teaching on the subject. I received it like I received salvation—by faith alone.

When I was about to make a decision for Christ, my natural mind could not comprehend how someone dying two thousand years ago could affect me at that moment. Therefore, for the first time in my life, I had to receive something by faith without understanding. It was and will always be an example of the first great principle of Christianity—receiving (believing) before seeing. So, on that April night of 1980, I put into practice what I had learned about salvation, going beyond natural thinking and heading into a spiritual dimension. It worked the same way as salvation, and that night as I knelt beside by bed, this mighty river of living water began to flow out of me.

That one decision has dramatically transformed the last thirty-three years of my personal life and ministry, launching me into the realm of supernatural power. I have been privileged over the years to watch the Holy Spirit move in mighty signs and wonders, healing the sick and destroying the works of the Devil.

The Devil, that cunning and crafty serpent of old, has been deceiving Christians into believing that this mighty tool passed away at the end of the first century. He has accomplished this through the traditions of men. He knows that this experience will change the way you see him, and he is terrified because he knows you will be powerful enough to affect the kingdom of darkness. It is pitiful that we sit Sunday after Sunday in what we wrongly describe as "church" and never see demons cast out of people or sick people cured. We call the power of God "weird" or describe people baptized with the Holy Ghost as being mystical or of the Devil. No wonder the Devil is laughing as he watches the body of Christ divided over the one tool that will break his back!

What's behind the door?

I learned a valuable lesson from the Holy Spirit concerning prophetic ministry or speaking for God. I was in my home church, and the Lord showed me four individuals that He wanted me to lay hands on and pray for. I got permission from the pastor to call them forward, and after I had prayed for them, the Lord began to give me more people to pray for.

This is what I call *progressive revelation*. When I acted on the first thing by faith rather than reason, the revelation and miracle door opened up, and whatever was behind the door came forward. We can see this in the Bible through the ministry of Philip.

> Now an angel of the Lord spoke to Philip, saying, "Arise and go toward the south along the road which goes down from Jerusalem to Gaza." This is desert. So he arose and went. And behold, a man of Ethiopia, a eunuch of great authority under Candace the queen of the Ethiopians, who had charge of all her treasury, and had come to Jerusalem to worship, was returning. And sitting in his chariot, he was reading Isaiah the prophet. Then the Spirit said to Philip, "Go near and overtake this chariot." So Philip ran to him, and heard him reading the prophet Isaiah, and said, "Do you understand what you are reading?" (Acts 8:26–30)

The angel of the Lord spoke to Philip and told him to go south. He didn't tell him why; He just told him to go. Philip acted on the angel's word, and when he got to where he met the man of Ethiopia, the Holy Spirit gave him the rest of the instructions. What if Philip had not gone? If he hadn't gone, he wouldn't have had the experience! He went, not because of reason or intellect, but by faith!

You will never experience or apply the tools that are available through the baptism of the Holy Spirit with the evidence of speaking in tongues if you are using your intellect or reasoning powers. You didn't come to Jesus by intellect and reason; you came to Him by faith. Faith soars above the natural to the spiritual; intellect keeps you grounded. The baptism of the Holy Spirit with the evidence of speaking in tongues does not make me better than you, but I am better off since I received it.

The Devil does not want you to have this gift, promise, experience, and tool. This deceiver knows that this tool has a powerful consequence on his kingdom of darkness. You will see his deception firsthand as we proceed.

Can you live without this gift and promise? Absolutely! However, I find no biblical precedent for turning down any gift or promise of God. I have another question for you. Are you willing to soar above the clouds and enter a dimension that will dramatically affect the way you live and minister to others? The choice is yours. You can either head toward the south road like Philip did, or you can just stay where you are!

The great joy in my life is to minister to "sponges." A "sponge" is one who soaks up the living water presented to them. I would rather sit in a room with ten sponges than in a great hall with ten thousand people who hear and do not understand, or see and do not perceive. Are you one of them, or are you a sponge? It will not be this book that changes you. It will be the Word of God, written and shared throughout this book, that will change you. In the end, it will be your faith that causes you to jump into this river of living water. Jesus desires that you experience these rivers of living water that flow out of the throne of God to water your spirit and bring power to your life!

Think of each chapter in this book as a key. Keys unlock and lock doors. If you never unlock the door to the baptism of the Holy Spirit with the evidence of speaking in tongues, then you will never see what is behind the door. This is a door that conceals not a onetime experience but a lifetime of experiences!

Come on in. The water's fine!

FAITH AND THE SPIRIT REALM

Christianity is a spiritual dimension.

Let me say that again. *Christianity is a spiritual dimension.* We often forget that everything we receive from God comes from another dimension: the dimension of the spirit realm.

The Holy Spirit comes to live in us when we are born from above. Now, we have a natural life and a spiritual life.

> There was a man of the Pharisees named Nicodemus, a ruler of the Jews. This man came to Jesus by night and said to Him, "Rabbi, we know that You are a teacher come from God; for no one can do these signs that You do unless God is with him."
>
> Jesus answered and said to him, "Most assuredly, I say to you, unless one is born again, he cannot *see* the kingdom of God."
>
> Nicodemus said to Him, "How can a man be born when he is old? Can he enter a second time into his mother's womb and be born?"

> Jesus answered, "Most assuredly, I say to you, unless one is born of water and the Spirit, he cannot *enter* the kingdom of God. That which is born of the flesh is flesh, and that which is *born of the Spirit* is spirit. Do not marvel that I said to you, 'You must be born again.' The wind blows where it wishes, and you hear the sound of it, but cannot tell where it comes from and where it goes. So is everyone who is born of the Spirit." (John 3:1–8, emphasis added)

Nicodemus was a religious, not a spiritual, man. Nicodemus approached Jesus at night instead of during the day. Was he trying to hide from his fellow Pharisees, worrying about what they would think? Do we do that today when we approach subjects like the Spirit's baptism or other spiritual gifts? Do we worry about what people will think? Have you grown up in "church" all of your life and never seen a demonstration of the Spirit and of power? Is the Christian life for you a series of religious acts?

Nicodemus recognized that Jesus was a teacher sent from God, because no one could do these spiritual demonstrations of healing and miracles unless God was with him. God was with Jesus in the person of the Holy Spirit, living in Him and moving through Him.

The Spirit that anointed Jesus is the same Spirit living in you—if you are born-again. "Men of Israel, hear these words: Jesus of Nazareth, a Man *attested* by God to you by miracles, wonders, and signs which God did through Him in your midst, as you yourselves also know" (Acts 2:22).

The meaning of the word *attested* points away from self and toward another. It indicates proof by demonstration. The miracles and signs proved that Jesus was a man sent from God and that this spirit realm was now manifesting (revealing) its power in the natural realm.

If I buy an AM radio, I have access to whatever stations are transmitted by AM wave frequency. If I add an FM receiver, then I pick up a whole new set of stations. In John 3:1–8, Jesus answered Nicodemus by telling him that the born-again experience allowed one to see and enter into the kingdom of God.

The Holy Spirit living in you is the FM receiver, which now receives transmissions from heaven and conveys them to you, in both thought and actions. Now, we have established that there is a vast difference between the natural (earthly) and the spiritual (kingdom of God). Jesus answered Nicodemus by telling him that the born-again experience allowed one to see and enter into the kingdom of God.

The other day, I spoke to an atheist at my favorite coffee shop. Instead of asking me about God, he made a lot of statements concerning his view of the Bible and God. His entire perspective was based on his natural view of things. I tried to explain to him, without showing an arrogant attitude, that Christianity is a spiritual dimension. Although I wasn't able to penetrate his theology of God, I knew that without the spiritual receiver (Holy Ghost), his view would never change!

As I left, the Lord gave me a vision concerning my meeting. I saw this young man writing questions on a blank wall. On the other side of the wall, God was writing the answers in the exact locations of the questions. The only thing that prevented the man from knowing the answers was the closed door between the two sides.

That door represented the entrance into God's kingdom. "I am the door. If anyone enters by Me, he will be saved, and will go in and out and find pasture. The thief does not come except to steal, and to kill, and to destroy. I have come that they may have life, and that they may have it more abundantly" (John 10:9–10).

You were born into a natural world. Almost every view and experience you have is based on this natural life. In fact, it is possible to go to church every Sunday and experience only the natural side of Christianity. "But the natural man does not receive the things of the Spirit of God, for they are foolishness to him; nor can he know them, because they are spiritually discerned" (1 Corinthians 2:14).

Many will read this Scripture and think that the natural man is an unbeliever. Nevertheless, many Christians do not receive all of the attributes of the Holy Ghost, such as the Spirit's baptism and the gifts of the Holy Spirit. The power of God has to be spiritually discerned. *Discernment* means to examine or investigate. When anyone refuses to examine the Scriptures concerning the power of God, those Scriptures are rendered absurd or silly. Many people are comfortable being natural but afraid of being supernatural. Their traditions block them from knowing this power that is available to *all* Christians.

It is not natural for you to perform beyond natural demonstrations. In fact, you cannot do this, for it is the Spirit of the Lord that does them through you (2 Corinthians 4:7). This is one of the main reasons that the Holy Spirit (above natural) came to live in you (natural). Americans are raised on rationalism, a creation of the eighteenth-century Age of Enlightenment. The Bible went one way, and science went the other. We need a logical answer to everything, which is in opposition to faith and the kingdom of God.

God does not run on logic. He runs on faith. Without faith, it is impossible to please Him, for those that come to Him must *believe* that He is and that He is a rewarder of them that diligently seek Him (Hebrews 11:6).

Doubting Thomas

> Now Thomas, called the Twin, one of the twelve, was not with them when Jesus came. The other disciples therefore said to him, "We have seen the Lord."
> So he said to them, "Unless I see in His hands the print of the nails, and put my finger into the print of the nails, and put my hand into His side, I will not believe."
> And after eight days His disciples were again inside, and Thomas with them. Jesus came, the doors being shut, and stood in the midst, and said, "Peace to you!" Then He said to Thomas, "Reach your finger here, and look at My hands; and reach your hand here, and put it into My side. Do not be unbelieving, but believing."
> And Thomas answered and said to Him, "My Lord and my God!"
> Jesus said to him, "Thomas, because you have seen Me, you have believed. Blessed are those who have not seen and yet have believed." (John 20:24–29)

Verse 27 says, "Do not be unbelieving, but believing." Access to all the spiritual blessings in the heavenlies is a result of believing, or receiving by faith before you see. Jesus was gracious to Thomas, and Thomas learned a valuable lesson that day. The only hindrance to your Christianity is your unbelief in what God's Word says. Everything I have obtained from that dimension has started with faith, through which I have then received, or taken hold of, His promises.

All Christianity begins with a step of faith, believing before you receive. Eventually, biblical knowledge fueled by experience produces understanding. Knowledge alone is not enough. You can read about the love of God and listen to messages about that love. But until you take a step of faith and open your heart to the reality and experience of the love of God, you have very little understanding of the depth and power of His great love. The more you pursue that love, the greater the understanding.

Observation and natural intellect have limitations. The dimension of the spirit realm eventually requires that you experience it. When you experience that realm within the context of the Bible, then the experience becomes truth. However, the truth does not necessarily have to agree with your intellect; nor should your intellect override the truth of the spiritual experience. Eventually, you bring your natural man into alignment with your spiritual man. The ultimate outcome is you become naturally supernatural!

Wrong Reasoning

> Now when His disciples had come to the other side, they had forgotten to take bread. Then Jesus said to them, "Take heed and beware of the leaven of the Pharisees and the Sadducees."
>
> And they reasoned among themselves, saying, "It is because we have taken no bread."

> But Jesus, being aware of it, said to them, "O you of little faith, why do you *reason* among yourselves because you have brought no bread? Do you not yet understand, or remember the five loaves of the five thousand and how many baskets you took up? Nor the seven loaves of the four thousand and how many large baskets you took up? How is it you do not understand that I did not speak to you concerning bread?—but to beware of the leaven of the Pharisees and Sadducees." Then they understood that He did not tell them to beware of the leaven of bread, but of the doctrine of the Pharisees and Sadducees. (Matthew 16:5–12, emphasis added)

Reason is not a bad thing, but reason can get in the way of the spiritual realm. Reason is only based on what you know. When something is presented to you, either by thought or demonstration, if it is unknown to the mind, then the mind goes in search of what it knows. If the answer is not found in the mind, then the person has the choice to abandon the thought or to pursue the answer. Sometimes the explanation is right in front of us in God's Word. At other times, we must, like the disciples in Matthew 16:5–12, allow the Lord to train us.

Twenty-six years ago, the Lord woke me up at 4:30 a.m. and told me to go out into the living room. I sat down on the couch, and it was the only time in my Christian walk when I sensed that "with you" and "in you" of John 14:17. It literally felt like He was standing in the room, speaking directly to me. He told me that He was going to teach me everything there was to know about spiritual gifts. I didn't ask Him why or how, I just received what He said by faith and went back to sleep. He has since performed what He said He'd do, with exceedingly abundant teaching and demonstration.

Christians who do not believe in spiritual power seldom ask the Holy Spirit to show them the truth. They are locked into their traditions and are afraid to venture further. The leaven (doctrine and traditions) of the Pharisees attacks their faith, and doubt sets in.

I have discipled many people in the "spirituals," the invisible powers from God. Those who grasp these spiritual powers have abandoned their former traditions and locked themselves on to the Word of God and the ministry of the Holy Spirit. Jesus is not a two-faced liar. He can't promise something to one person that He doesn't promise to all. If He says you will speak in new tongues if you believe (Mark 16:17), He means it!

The Kingdom of God

"Then He said, 'To what shall we liken the kingdom of God? Or with what parable shall we picture it? It is like a mustard seed which, when it is sown on the ground, is smaller than all the seeds on earth; but when it is sown, it grows up and becomes greater than all herbs, and shoots out large branches, so that the birds of the air may nest under its shade'" (Mark 4:30–33).

The mustard seed is the size of a printed period on a page, yet it grows into a tree where the birds of the air can nest in its shade! This seed was designed by God to produce the same kind of tree every time it is planted. All one has to do is plant it in the soil and walk away. That is natural growth.

Spiritual growth works the same way. Whenever we plant our faith on the solid rock of God's Word, it is designed to work the same way every time. If I plant my faith on the promise of receiving the spirituals, and that faith does not waver, then I will receive what I planted. Abraham did not waver over the promises of God, and neither should you!

When a farmer plants a seed in the ground, he doesn't dig it up a few hours later. The Devil will always try to dig up your seed of faith before it has a chance to take root: "Another parable He put forth to them, saying: 'The kingdom of heaven is like a man who sowed good seed in his field; but while men slept, his enemy came and sowed tares among the wheat and went his way. But when the grain had sprouted and produced a crop, then the tares also appeared'" (Matthew 13:24–26).

The power I received from the Holy Spirit and from the kingdom of God has given me the opportunity to wreak havoc on the kingdom of darkness. The power of God is the one thing that the Serpent does not want in your arsenal. The traditions of men, doubt, tares, leaven, and any other misdirection will be used by him to prevent you from a powerful, victorious life.

> "I do not pray for these alone, but also for those who will believe in Me through their word; that they all may be one, as You, Father, are in Me, and I in You; that they also may be *one in Us*, that the world may believe that You sent Me. And the glory which You gave Me I have given them, that they may be *one just as We are one*: I in them, and You in Me; that they may be made perfect in one, and that the world may know that You have sent Me, and have loved them as You have loved Me." (John 17:20–23, emphasis added)

The Holy Spirit lives with me and in me (John 14:16–17). There is one Holy Spirit who lives in all of us. We know that there are not hundreds of millions of Holy Spirits living in born-again Christians, but our understanding is not fully clear on how this miraculous habitation exists.

Yet Jesus makes it clear that we are one with the Trinity! We are not of the same divine nature as the triune God, but we are in their image and likeness. We are connected to them in this spirit realm. We are "in Him." This is too marvelous for words or description. With that oneness comes communication. We get to walk with them every day of our lives. We have complete access to that spirit realm and all of the wonderful blessings that come with that union.

I can feel them around me every day. I walk with the Trinity and talk with the Trinity. I know that they are there, ready to help me in every aspect of my life. The Holy Spirit is my best spiritual friend, and He gives me all the juice I need to accomplish His purposes. The world and all its darkness will soon be fading away. The Son of righteousness is about to rise with healing in His wings. The King of Kings and the Lord of Lords will soon mount His white horse and establish His kingdom on this earth!

Fix your eyes squarely on Him. Become familiar with this glorious realm of the kingdom of God. Do not allow one tare—not even one—to touch your spiritual crop. Come and join the Spirit as He introduces you to the spiritual blessings in the heavenlies!

"While we do not look at the things which are seen, but at the things which are not seen. For the things which are seen are temporary, but the things which are not seen are eternal" (2 Corinthians 4:18).

MY STORY

My conversion experience was powerful. On the third Sunday in October, 1979, I woke up at 6:00 a.m. in the front seat of my car—covered in vomit. At 9:00 a.m., I was dressed in a suit and headed for church. In less than three hours, I had given my life to Jesus, experienced a physical manifestation of His power that had blown all of the residual alcohol out through the top of my head, and transformed me into a new creature in twenty seconds. From that moment on, I have never thought about drinking or been fully tempted. The Bible is true when it says that if the Son makes you free, you shall be free indeed! (John 8:36).

Since I had never read the Bible, this first encounter with the Lord was an encounter with power. Beyond any shadow of doubt, I realized that there existed a supernatural power that could invade this world in an instant. It was a power so awesome and unbelievable that it took a two-and-a-half-mile walk to church that morning to completely absorb what had just occurred! That same morning, the Lord restored my marriage and brought my wife and me into a loving and biblical relationship until her death on Mother's Day in 1997.

I began to attend the Lancaster Congregational Church in Lancaster, Massachusetts. The pastor was a wonderful and gentle man. He taught a Bible study every Sunday morning, and I made it a goal to be there and learn about the Bible. I was hungry and wanted to learn all I could about this thing called Christianity.

In the spring of 1980, just six months after my conversion experience, I attended a meeting where two women were talking about the gifts of the Holy Spirit. I can remember very little about what they said, except that the baptism with the Holy Spirit was a powerful experience that would change my spiritual life.

When we got home from the meeting, my wife Barbara went to bed, but I had a few things to do before I went upstairs. Eventually I headed toward the bedroom. All of a sudden, I stopped in the middle of the hall and thought about what the two women had said. It was a giant leap to go from being born-again to speaking in a spiritual language. The only time I'd heard that language, I'd gotten scared.

However, if this was a legitimate gift and promise from God, why would I not want it? I had never read the book of Acts or any other place in the Bible about "speaking in tongues" and this infilling of the Holy Spirit. Something compelled me to go into our guest bedroom and give it a shot, so I knelt down by the side of the bed and got ready.

My first question was, "What if it doesn't work?" Then the recollection of my born-again experience came before me. The question then was, "How can someone dying two thousand years ago affect me today?" Now the answer came. Salvation worked, so this should work too.

I realized that I could not just open my mouth and start speaking English. I asked Jesus to baptize me with the Holy Spirit, as He is the One who does that (John 1:33), and I asked the Holy Spirit to give me the utterance. My mouth opened, and out came this foreign spiritual language. My whole body felt like every cell was filled with electrical power. Then I lay down on the bed, and something that felt like some form of spiritual lightning proceeded to flash from my toes to the top of my head for about thirty minutes. Wow! It was real, and I'd gotten more than I'd bargained for.

Drunk Behind the Paint Cans

The next day, I arrived for work at Sears, and the spiritual lightning had turned into giant Alka Seltzer tablets. Everything inside me was bubbling up and heading for my mouth. It got so bad that I had to run into the warehouse every couple of hours, hide behind the paint cans, and just speak in tongues.

The bright idea came to me to share this with my running partner, whom I'd trained with for the Boston Marathon. Heading for his office, I ran into him in an extremely narrow aisle, leaving him less than a foot away from me. He wasn't a Christian, but that did not matter to me. The rivers of living waters were flowing, and I did more than share. I said, "Hey, Charlie, watch this!" When I began to speak in tongues, he looked like Wile E. Coyote before the bomb exploded on him.

The immediate benefit of this spiritual baptism was a greater awareness of the Devil and the spiritual world of demons. Another benefit was the power of the Holy Spirit making it feel like a spiritual Corvette engine was turned on within my spirit. There was a new boldness and a new sense of the presence of the Holy Spirit living in me and through me.

When I went back to my church, I told the pastor what had happened. He said that they didn't do that in the church. Welcome to the world of the traditions of men and denominationalism! I was dumbfounded. He believed in it, but they didn't practice it in the church. There were too many people opposed to it. This was my first introduction to the traditions of men nullifying the Word of God. I will always be grateful to the Holy Spirit for branding me with this power. Once it happened, no man or tradition would ever intimidate me into thinking that the experience was not real.

In 1984 I was led by the Holy Spirit to transfer to a Pentecostal church. We use the expression *Pentecostal* to refer to a church or denomination where speaking in tongues is accepted. Not too long after I arrived, they decided to add a new educational wing to the church. Included in these plans was a prayer room. Once it was built, five or six of us decided to meet every morning to pray for our church and for revival.

So at 6:00 a.m., Monday through Friday, we stormed the spiritual realm, using our spiritual language to pray in the Holy Spirit, knowing that He, the Spirit, was listening to every word we spoke. Then, after a year and a half, the answer came from Him.

Turning Out the Sunday School Class

A friend of mine invited us and another couple over to his house for dinner. After dinner, I prayed for the host's daughter, and she "fell out" under the power of God.

When a person "falls out" under the power of God, they are not able to stand. Pentecostals use the expression *slain in the Spirit*. I do not like the word *slain*, because it means "killed." When the glory of the Lord resonates inside you to a high degree, the electrical impulses in your muscles shut off, and you fall down.

The room suddenly became saturated with His presence. Eventually, we moved to the kitchen to leave, and after another two and half hours in the kitchen, we left. God's presence was so strong that it was hard to talk or move. I was grateful to God for another powerful evening with the Holy Ghost as master of ceremonies.

The next morning, while I was taking a shower, the Holy Spirit told me that He was going to "turn out the Sunday school class." I knew that lingo; it meant that He was going to demonstrate His power and shake them up. Right after He said that, He filled me with a fresh infilling of His presence, and I shouted. All my spiritual engines were revved up and ready to go!

When I got to the Sunday school room, I noticed that two of the people who had been with me the other night were also in attendance. They looked like they had been struck by the same power. I knew that the Spirit was about to turn me loose. Then the moment came. I asked the Sunday school teacher if I could pray for someone. She said yes, and the floodgates opened.

The first woman I prayed for was very pregnant. I called her up to the front and spoke something over her, and she went down under the power of the Spirit. Then I called her husband up, and he fell out and was lying over her legs. Then I called another woman up and spoke over her life. She turned around, walked five paces back, and started waving her hands in the air.

By now, the Sunday school teacher looked flustered. Her class presentation had just gone down the tubes. This was one of the women who had attended our prayer meetings to pray for an outpouring of the Holy Spirit. Now it was happening, and she was not aware of the Spirit's direction!

Then I saw a girl sitting in the first pew. I told her that she wanted the baptism of the Holy Spirit with the evidence of speaking in tongues. She nodded her head yes, jumped out of her seat, and ran forward. I laid hands on her head, and she immediately spoke in tongues. What a wild scene that was. Two were out on the floor, one was waving her hands, and another was speaking in the Spirit. Then I noticed the Sunday school leader standing in the entrance. He had his watch off and was pointing to it, telling me that the class was over. The class was over, and the power of the Holy Spirit was quenched!

When we left and went to the main sanctuary, I saw my wife pacing back and forth in front of the pulpit. She was praying in the Spirit, unaware of what was going on around her. For my wife to do that was nothing short of a miracle. My wife was a quiet and reserved person, not given to any public displays. The Holy Spirit was invading both the Sunday school class and the main service.

Then the leadership arrived through the side door, the music started, and the Holy Ghost was quenched for a second time. It was all over. I knew that if the leadership had recognized that the Holy Spirit wanted preeminence in the service, we might have seen something spectacular.

The next Sunday, the Sunday school leader stopped me before Sunday school class. He told me that both he and the pastor agreed that the Holy Spirit could only move in the sanctuary and not in the Sunday school class. I told them that they were nuts! Then I told him that it was highly unlikely that they would ever see Him demonstrate His power again in any of the rooms. I also found it bizarre that the Sunday school teacher, who had also prayed for a moving of the Spirit, had not recognized the work of the Spirit in her class.

That was the beginning of the end for Barbara and me at the church. Our time eventually came to move on as directed by the Spirit. If that church's programs and traditions had been laid aside for that one Sunday, I believe they would have seen more than they ever could have prayed for. Because of their unbelief, they saw very little from that point on. However, I was still blessed by the spiritual times in those morning prayer meetings while praying in the Holy Ghost.

The baptism of the Holy Spirit with the evidence of speaking in tongues is not just a tool for prayer. I discovered that it was also a tool to be used in the midst of demonic warfare.

The Girl with the Ten-Foot Lizard

In 1991 I was finishing up a tent meeting, when a young girl approached me and said that she needed deliverance. I said I was willing to help her, but we never connected after that. However, almost two years later, I would meet her in an atmosphere of demonic violence.

One day my pastor called me and asked me to come to our church and help him and some others to deliver this girl from demonic spirits. They had already tried the previous day but had been unsuccessful, so I agreed to show up that evening. Our church was located in an office building where we had rented two floors. They were not big rooms, but they were adequate for the size of our congregation. We decided it would be best if we used the room upstairs, and I arrived before the others brought the girl in.

I told the pastor that I was going to sit away from them and just observe (fat chance). One of the women came in carrying a five-gallon pail and a 3-by-5-foot mat. I asked her what they were for, and she said that the other night the girl had thrown up some stuff and that the demon had thrown her to the carpet and run her face across it. Wow! It sounded exciting, and I was hoping for some action.

Then the others brought the girl in. She was barely five feet tall and probably weighed about 105 pounds, soaking wet. They sat her in a chair and began to talk to her. I was about fifteen feet to her right, but she was not looking toward me.

Then the Holy Spirit told me that when her eyes turned and looked at me, complete mayhem was going to break forth. And that was exactly what happened.

She turned and looked at me and immediately kicked the pail with her foot. It shot across the room like a guided missile, and then the three of them grabbed her and threw her facedown on the mat. I jumped out of my seat, ran over to her right side, and grabbed her arm. It took the strength of all four of us to hold her down. The pastor was a weight lifter, and I was fairly strong for my age.

She started to growl and then tried to push herself up off the floor. I was kneeling next to her had both of my arms locked and pressing down on her right arm. She began to lift her arm up off the floor, and that took superhuman strength.

Then I put my face down to the floor and began to speak to the demon that had control of her. She turned her face away from me because the eyes are the gateway to the soul. When she turned back to face me, the pupils of her eyes turned into lizard's slits. It was wild, just like seeing someone's face morph in a movie.

I told the demon within her that it must leave, but the demon said it was going to kill me. I just said, "Nah. Wrong answer!" This battle went back and forth for some time.

Then I began to pray in the Holy Spirit. This warfare language came out of me, and then the Holy Spirit gave me instructions. He said to tell everyone to let her go.

What? If we let her go in this condition, she could throw a couple of us out the second-story window. She was lying on the mat they had brought, and the Holy Spirit told me to bind her to that mat with authority. "And from the days of John the Baptist until now the kingdom of heaven suffers violence, and the violent take it by force" (Matthew 11:12).

Kingdom violence must be met with kingdom authority. Demons always deal in territory and authority. They will do anything to intimidate you and make you fear them. But when the Holy Spirit gives you instructions, then He will give you the power to fulfill His instructions.

I told them to let her go. They looked at me a little funny, not sure whether I had lost my mind, but they obeyed. Then I pointed my finger at the girl and verbally bound the evil spirit to the mat.

The demon tried to move her up and off the carpet but without success. Once that spirit realized that it had lost the power encounter, it was intimidated and weakened. I commanded it to come out of her, and she fell over like a dead person. Sometimes people will be knocked out by the violent force of a demon leaving.

When she came to her senses, she was free. We led her in a salvation prayer, and she became born-again. While she was sitting there on the carpet, she began to look straight ahead as if she was seeing something. I asked her what she was looking at, and she replied that she could see the demon standing on the other side of the room. Boy, would I have paid money to see that! I asked her what it looked like, and she stated that it was a ten-foot lizard with a tail running down the rest of the room.

I told her that she was now a child of God and had the authority to command that demon to go back to the Abyss. She commanded it to leave. After a brief moment, she began to giggle. I asked her what had happened, and she said that two angels had come down, grabbed that freaky thing, and flown off with him. That experience was about the best entertainment I'd had all year!

I am not making light of the encounter. I am telling you that there is an exhilaration that takes place when the power of the Holy Spirit is magnified inside you. The glory rises, and spiritual language produces a .357 Magnum pistol, and the Enemy gets blown away. As the Scripture says, "Behold, I give you the authority to trample [put your foot on and hold down, treat something with contempt and insult] on serpents and scorpions, and over all the power of the enemy, and nothing shall by any means hurt you" (Luke 10:19).

There is one more story that I want to share with you concerning this glorious experience of tongues. It's a story that confronts the traditions of men and the legalism that goes with it.

Filled with Her Pants On

I am always fascinated by the ministry of the Holy Spirit when He is in one of His entertaining moods. Such was the case at a church service in Rhode Island. Now, don't get religious on me! We were created in the image of God. He can get angry, and He can laugh or grieve. Granted, His nature is divine, but laughter is still the best medicine.

In my senior year at Bible school, I was invited to preach at a local church in the area. I had never met the pastor or attended any of the services. At that time, most of my services followed a somewhat predictable course. First came the preaching of the Word of God, and then came whatever the Holy Ghost decided.

Frequently, I would be directed by the Spirit to begin praying for people. The Holy Spirit would use the prophetic gifting on my life to pray for the sick and to minister in the gifts of the Holy Spirit. I would instruct the ushers to bring up at least ten or fifteen people at a time. Moving all the way to my right and ministering to each individual, I worked my way down the line.

This was one of the first occasions where the pastor and the assistant pastor stood right by me so they could verify what I was saying to the people. I wasn't used to this, but I accepted it without hesitation.

After praying for the first group of people, the ushers brought up another ten to fifteen people. I made my way down to the end of the line again, ready to repeat the process. Out of the corner of my eye, I noticed a young girl in black pants, staring intently at me. Then the Spirit told me that she wanted to be baptized with the Holy Spirit and speak in tongues.

I pointed to her and said, "You want the baptism with the Holy Spirit." She nodded yes, jumped out of her seat, and ran up to the front. I put my hand on her head, and she immediately spoke in this beautiful spiritual language.

The whole congregation went bananas! You would have thought that someone had just been raised from the dead. Many were laughing and crying. However, the facial expression on the assistant pastor had gone from joyful to cold. The pastor, on the other hand, was just smiling and laughing under his breath.

After the service, I joined the pastor in his study. Once the door was closed, he just laughed and said, "She got filled with her pants on!" I thought he had lost his mind. With great joy in his heart, he explained his statement.

The young girl had been trying for months to receive the baptism with the Holy Spirit. The assistant pastor, who came from a legalistic denomination, had told everyone that the reason the girl had not received that gift was because she wore pants to church! Talk about killing two birds with one stone!

There is more to this gift than just the initial experience. A life lived in the Spirit is an exciting life. I put the key in the door and received all that was behind it. There have been hundreds of wonderful spiritual experiences in my life that are a direct result of my baptism by the Holy Spirit with the evidence of speaking in tongues.

I do not guarantee that this experience will produce lightning when you receive it. However, the promise is that you will receive this miraculous power. Those are not my words; they are the words of the Master in Acts 1:8: "But you shall receive power when the Holy Spirit has come upon you; and you shall be witnesses to Me in Jerusalem, and in all Judea and Samaria, and to the end of the earth."

HISTORICAL EVENTS BEFORE THE DAY OF PENTECOST

There are certain key events in biblical history that have shaped my understanding of the baptism of the Holy Spirit with the evidence of speaking in tongues. Some are stories, and some are prophetic announcements. All have influenced the way I approach the baptism of the Holy Spirit.

The Tower of Babel

> Now the whole earth had one language and one speech. And it came to pass, as they journeyed from the east, that they found a plain in the land of Shinar, and they dwelt there. Then they said to one another, "Come, let us make bricks and bake them thoroughly." They had brick for stone, and they had asphalt for mortar. And they said, "Come, let us build ourselves a city, and a tower whose top is in the heavens; let us make

a name for ourselves, lest we be scattered abroad over the face of the whole earth."

But the Lord came down to see the city and the tower which the sons of men had built. And the Lord said, "Indeed the people are one and they all have one language, and this is what they begin to do; now nothing that they propose to do will be withheld from them. Come, let Us go down and there confuse their language, that they may not understand one another's speech." So the Lord scattered them abroad from there over the face of all the earth, and they ceased building the city. Therefore its name is called Babel, because there the Lord confused the language of all the earth; and from there the Lord scattered them abroad over the face of all the earth. (Genesis 11:1–9)

This would be the last time in human history when all the inhabitants of the earth would speak one language. In the plains of Shinar, the land located in southern Mesopotamia (modern day Iraq and Syria), a king named Nimrod was hard at work, building a tower whose top was to reach the heavens; or so he thought. His people wanted to make a name for themselves, building a structure that would reach to the heavens.

History is full of men who had lofty goals and grand illusions. They were prideful men who, like Lucifer, tried to elevate themselves to a position of equality with God. They are all gone now, and God still sits on the throne of heaven without equal. The leaders of Babel feared that they would be scattered throughout the whole earth, which was exactly what God desired.

"Then God blessed them, and God said to them, 'Be fruitful and multiply; fill the earth and subdue it; have dominion over the fish of the sea, over the birds of the air, and over every living thing that moves on the earth" (Genesis 1:28).

They wanted to stay together in one place, but God's original command was to fill the earth. Guess who won? The God who had said "Let us make man in our own image" decided that it was time to put an end to their folly. Now He said, "Let us go down there and confuse their language."

As opposed to the disobedience demonstrated at the Tower of Babel, the disciples were obedient in waiting in the Upper Room for the promise of the Father. Instead of remaining in one place, their commission was to take their experience of tongues and power to Jerusalem, Judea, Samaria, and the ends of the earth.

"For as the body is one and has many members, but all the members of that one body, being many, are one body, so also is Christ. For by *one Spirit we were all baptized into one body*—whether Jews or Greeks, whether slaves or free—and have all been made *to drink into one Spirit*. For in fact the body is not one member but many" (1 Corinthians 12:12–14, emphasis added).

The baptism of the Holy Spirit with the evidence of speaking in tongues was the normal experience of their day as opposed to the controversial way we treat this experience today. The Holy Spirit supplies rivers of living water, the living water that we drink for spiritual nourishment and vitality! I believe that Paul was speaking of the Spirit's baptism when he said, "For by one Spirit we are all baptized into one body."

There was great unity among Christians in the first century because of their experience of speaking in different tongues. It started with the Jews in Acts 2 and reached out to the Gentiles in Acts 10.

Today, there is no unity concerning this biblical doctrine. However, this changes neither the experience nor the truth of Scripture! The experience today is just the same as it was two thousand years ago. Jesus is the same yesterday, today, and forever (Hebrews 13:8). Jesus and the Holy Spirit are still baptizing believers today into this wonderful and powerful infilling.

The Prophecy of Joel

"Be glad then, you children of Zion, and rejoice in the Lord your God; for He has given you the former rain faithfully, and He will cause the rain to come down for you—the former rain, and the latter rain in the first month" (Joel 2:23).

The latter rain would fall in the Jews' first month, which was called Nisan (April). The former rain would come six months prior, at seedtime. There is a natural seedtime and harvest, and there is a spiritual seedtime and harvest. The prophetic words spoken by Joel would activate the spiritual seeds in the latter rain and the outpouring of the Holy Spirit on the day of Pentecost.

"And it shall come to pass afterward that I will pour out My Spirit on all flesh; your sons and your daughters shall prophesy, your old men shall dream dreams, your young men shall see visions. And also on My menservants and on My maidservants I will pour out My Spirit in those days" (Joel 2:28–29). Joel prophesied that the Holy Spirit would be poured out (burst forth in a large quantity) on all flesh. Every tongue, tribe, and nation on the earth would have the opportunity to receive this outpouring.

Sons and daughters would prophesy by speaking forth revelation from the heart of God in words of wisdom and knowledge that would bring edification, exhortation, and comfort to many. This outpouring included sons, daughters, old men, young men, menservants, and maidservants, and it was never limited to any age, gender, or race. The only limitation was belief.

Old men would dream dreams and young men would see visions. Dreams and visions are a method God uses to communicate with His people, whether they are sleeping or awake. The dreams and visions included the raising up of the New Testament prophetic ministry that would accompany this outpouring. We will see that it was through vision that this outpouring came to the Gentiles at Cornelius' house (Acts 10:44).

The time period we live in is included in the last days. We are two thousand years closer to seeing the second coming than Peter was on the day of Pentecost.

The Prophecy of Jesus

"On the last day, that great day of the feast, Jesus stood and cried out, saying, 'If anyone thirsts, let him come to Me and drink. He who believes in Me, as the Scripture has said, out of his heart will flow rivers of living water.' But this He spoke concerning the Spirit, whom those believing in Him would receive; for the Holy Spirit was not yet given, because Jesus was not yet glorified" (John 7:37–39).

The word *tabernacle* in the Hebrew is *mishkan*. *Mishkan* is a dwelling place or tent (tabernacle) of meeting. We know from Scripture that the Lord visited Moses in Exodus 33:9, bringing His cloud of glory and speaking to him face-to-face. The Feast of Tabernacles was a celebration of Israel's wandering in the wilderness, sheltered by God's provision and direction.

Whenever I think of the word *tabernacle*, I think of Moses' encounter with God in the tent of meeting. What a glorious event that must have been!

"And it came to pass, when Moses entered the tabernacle, that the pillar of cloud descended and stood at the door of the tabernacle, and the Lord talked with Moses. All the people saw the pillar of cloud standing at the tabernacle door, and all the people rose and worshiped, each man in his tent door. So the Lord spoke to Moses face to face, as a man speaks to his friend. And he would return to the camp, but his servant Joshua the son of Nun, a young man, did not depart from the tabernacle" (Exodus 33:9–11).

The Glory That Excels

"For if the ministry of condemnation had glory, the ministry of righteousness exceeds much more in glory. For even what was made glorious had no glory in this respect, because of the glory that excels. For if what is passing away was glorious, what remains is much more glorious" (2 Corinthians 3:9–11).

We can "feast" every day on the Holy Spirit living in us, living inside our tabernacle or temple (1 Corinthians 6:19). The glory lives within us. My life is centered on communicating face-to-face with the Spirit. He walks with me and talks with me. On occasion, He lights up my physical body with His glory. He is my best spiritual friend!

On the last (eighth) day of the Feast of Tabernacles, the priests formed a procession at the Pool of Siloam, gathered water from the pool into a symbolic golden pitcher, and then carried the pitcher back to the altar of the temple for a symbolic offering. This was a remembrance of God's provision of water in the wilderness, when water flowed out of a rock and provided refreshment to an entire nation. At the rise in the altar, the priest poured the water through a silver funnel that led to the base of the altar. The people gathered and then gave shouts of praise, giving glory to God.

During this particular Feast of Tabernacles, the stage was set for Jesus, the Master Prophet, to announce the coming of the Holy Spirit. There came a perfect moment for Jesus to speak, and He shouted out his message, for it was important to Him that everyone there—and in the ages to come—hear what He had to say. "'If anyone thirsts, let him come to Me and drink. He who believes in Me, as the Scripture has said, out of his heart will flow rivers of living water.' But this He spoke concerning the Spirit, whom those believing in Him would receive; for the Holy Spirit was not yet given, because Jesus was not yet glorified" (John 7:37–39).

The living water was the Holy Spirit coming to the 120 people in the upper room on the day of Pentecost. I have always thought that the sound they heard of a mighty rushing wind symbolized Jesus sitting down at the right hand of the Father. The Holy Spirit then rose out of Him and headed toward the upper room to fill all men with the same Spirit that had been in Jesus during His earthly ministry. It was living water flowing out of the Rock of our salvation that would and will bring refreshment to millions!

The Samaritan woman who met Jesus at Jacob's well asked Him for natural water. Jesus desired to give her spiritual water, water that causes one never to thirst again. His water is the fountain that springs forth into everlasting life. His water is the water that pours not from a pitcher into a basin but flows inside of each of us, causing the rivers to deepen (Ezekiel 47:1–9). He is the Man with the measuring stick, and whatever He measures increases.

Jesus was prophesying that a great river was about to be ignited by the coming of the Holy Spirit on the day of Pentecost. This river would flow through the desert valleys of thirsty men's souls, causing spiritual life to all who jumped into it. This river would cause many to be healed and delivered.

Prophetic Announcement of John the Baptist

Four times in the Gospels the prophet John the Baptist announced that there was One coming after him who would baptize, not with water but with the Holy Spirit. John also made the distinction between his role of baptizing with water and Jesus' role of baptizing with the Holy Spirit.

In those days, people marked their Christian salvation with water baptism, becoming *born of* the Spirit. The event on the day of Pentecost would mark the outpouring of the Holy Spirit, and speaking in tongues would demonstrate that a person was being *filled with* the Spirit. The Spirit's baptism is one of many "fillings" provided to believers to bring forth spiritual demonstrations.

Here are the four announcements recorded in the gospels.

"I indeed baptize you with water unto repentance, but He who is coming after me is mightier than I, whose sandals I am not worthy to carry. He will baptize you with the Holy Spirit and fire" (Matthew 3:11).

"I indeed baptized you with water, but He will baptize you with the Holy Spirit" (Mark 1:8).

"John answered, saying to all, 'I indeed baptize you with water; but One mightier than I is coming, whose sandal strap I am not worthy to loose. He will baptize you with the Holy Spirit and fire" (Luke 3:16).

"I did not know Him, but He who sent me to baptize with water said to me, 'Upon whom you see the Spirit descending, and remaining on Him, this is He who baptizes with the Holy Spirit'" (John 1:33).

Jesus' Words to His Disciples Prior to His Ascension

> Later He appeared to the eleven as they sat at the table; and He rebuked their unbelief and hardness of heart, because they did not believe those who had seen Him after He had risen. And He said to them, "Go into all the world and preach the gospel to every creature. He who believes and is baptized will be saved; but he who does not believe will be condemned. And these signs will follow those who believe: In My name they will cast out demons; they will speak with new tongues; they will take up serpents; and if they drink anything deadly, it will by no means hurt them; they will lay hands on the sick, and they will recover."
>
> So then, after the Lord had spoken to them, He was received up into heaven, and sat down at the right hand of God. And they went out and preached everywhere, the Lord working with them and confirming the word through the accompanying signs. Amen. (Mark 16:14–20)

I don't think I would like to start any meal with a rebuke from Jesus of Nazareth. The rebuke, a strong disapproval of their thinking, was based on their unbelief and drifting from the faith. He had to get them back to center, because He was about to give them instructions that could only be carried out by faith: a command to go into all the world and preach and baptize. Mark's account added some things to what Jesus said to His disciples before He departed. Jesus said that signs, miraculous manifestations, would accompany those who believed.

First, in His name the disciples would have the authority to cast out demons. So casting out demons is part of the Great Commission!

Second, in His name the disciples would speak in new tongues, which is the baptism with the Holy Spirit. So the baptism with the Holy Spirit is part of the Great Commission!

Third, the disciples would be protected from bodily harm from deadly drink or serpent venom (Acts 28:1–6). So divine protection is part of the Great Commission.

And fourth, the disciples would lay hands on the sick, and those who were sick would recover. So divine healing is part of the Great Commission.

Then the Lord was taken up, and what He said was put into action. The disciples went off to preach and to practice all that the Lord had commanded them. His stamp of authority and approval was on them, and the Lord confirmed their mission with signs and wonders.

So, here is my question. If some people believe that signs and wonders passed away at the close of the first century, then does that mean that the Great Commission also ceased? I believe it does cease for those who hold dear to their belief that signs and wonders are not for today. It is too late for me. I have already experienced the Lord working with me in signs and wonders.

This great evangelistic tool brought three thousand souls to the Lord on the day of Pentecost, and five thousand men believed as a result of the healing of the lame man in Acts 3. Jesus Himself gathered multitudes because of His ability to demonstrate God's power.

> The former account I made, O Theophilus, of all that Jesus began both to do and teach, until the day in which He was taken up, after He through the Holy Spirit had given commandments to the apostles whom He had chosen, to whom He also presented Himself alive after His suffering by many infallible proofs, being seen by them during forty days and speaking of the things pertaining to the kingdom of God. And being assembled together with them, He commanded them not to depart from Jerusalem, but to wait for the Promise of the Father, "which," He said, "you have heard from Me; for John truly baptized with water, but you shall be baptized with the Holy Spirit not many days from now." (Acts 1:1–5)

The command or charge was to go to Jerusalem and wait for the Promise (Holy Spirit) of the Father. The Commander of the universe charged His troops to go to Jerusalem and receive the power of the Holy Spirit. "But you shall receive [take possession of something in order to carry it away and make it your own] power [might, ability, strength, enablement, miracles] when the Holy Spirit has come upon you; and you shall be witnesses to Me in Jerusalem, and in all Judea and Samaria, and to the end of the earth" (Acts 1:8).

They were going to take hold of that power and send it to the ends of the earth! John baptized in water for repentance, and Jesus baptizes in the Holy Spirit for power. We have the privilege of receiving both. The good news is that this experience and power is still being carried to others today as they receive this glorious experience.

I lived the early part of my life in a town called Bala-Cynwyd, Pennsylvania. You can find it on a map, but if you have never experienced living there, it would be known to you in name only. The same holds true for this power you receive when you are baptized with the Holy Spirit with the evidence of speaking in tongues: you know it in name only. To truly understand what Jesus was saying about power, one has to experience it.

There is no ignorance as dangerous as experienced ignorance. Experienced ignorance means living under unbiblical doctrines and believing them to be the only truth. Given equal theology, a man with an experience is never at the mercy of a man with an argument. The supernatural manifestations of the Holy Spirit are fully understood when they are experienced, not argued.

ICE

"Yet now, brethren, I know that you did it in ignorance, as did also your rulers" (Acts 3:17).

Several years ago, I received a vision from the Lord. I saw an ice cube, and then the Holy Spirit gave me these letters: *I, C, E.*

I waited almost two weeks for more information, and then He filled in the blanks:

- Ignorance
- Control
- Experience

At first, I had some difficulty interpreting why the Spirit had given me this vision, but eventually these three words would play a major role in the operation of the power of God in the church and the church's resistance to this power. Ignorance is a lack of proper knowledge, and knowledge has a beginning, a process, and an end. Therefore, knowledge must be coupled with experience to grasp the fullness of what is being promised.

A disciple is a learner, one who follows the example and teachings of a teacher. The goal is to reproduce that teacher and his knowledge in the disciple. However, when the teacher omits or attacks, through religious doctrine, the power of God, then the disciple suffers the same fate as the teacher.

My experience has been that whoever controls the pulpit controls the service and the theology expressed. Control is not necessarily a negative thing, considering all the problems that were taking place in the Corinthian church. But controlling the ministry of the Holy Spirit is not what God designed the church to do. In most cases, fear is the overwhelming factor that restricts and eliminates the spirituals (activities of supernatural power).

Fear produces wrong thinking. Fear projects results before they happen. Fear weakens and quenches spiritual faith. Fear builds fences to keep some people in and other people out. One of the roots of fear is the lack of being able to control the atmosphere. If there is not a unity of faith in the assembly of believers, then the spirituals are hindered.

> That which was from the beginning, which we have heard, which we have seen with our eyes, which we have looked upon, and our hands have handled, concerning the Word of life—the life was manifested, and we have

> seen, and bear witness, and declare to you that eternal life which was with the Father and was manifested to us—that which we have seen and heard we declare to you, that you also may have fellowship with us; and truly our fellowship is with the Father and with His Son Jesus Christ. And these things we write to you that your joy may be full. (1 John 1:1–4)

How can we witness and declare the wonderful works of God if we have not experienced all that the Bible says we can experience? Does it really come down to biblical experience? One assembly experiences the prophetic gifts and another does not. One group says it is for today, and another group says it has ceased. It will never be my job to convince you of anything. What you believe determines the outcome, and the choice is yours.

Luke's Account of Jesus' Command

"Then He said to them, 'Thus it is written, and thus it was necessary for the Christ to suffer and to rise from the dead the third day, and that repentance and remission of sins should be preached in His name to all nations, beginning at Jerusalem. And you are witnesses of these things. Behold, I send the Promise of My Father upon you; but tarry in the city of Jerusalem until you are endued with power from on high" (Luke 24:46–49).

The baptism with the Holy Spirit is a gift. The baptism with the Holy Spirit is an experience. The baptism with the Holy Spirit is a tool. And the baptism with the Holy Spirit is a promise. A promise is a declaration that one is about to do or furnish something that is completely under the control of the declarer to fulfill. In fact, the Holy Spirit is called "the Promise" of the Father.

Jesus told them that they would be endued (mantled) with power. The word *endued* means "to put on a coat." Elijah's coat went to Elisha. The relationship between Elijah and Elisha was a forerunner to the relationship between Jesus and His disciples. (Read 1 Kings 19:16–21 and 2 Kings 2:1–18.)

- Elijah was a prophet, and Jesus was a prophet.
- Elijah was Elisha's mentor. Jesus was His disciples' mentor.
- Elijah went up into heaven and so did Jesus.
- Elijah's mantle (clothing of power) was passed to Elisha. Jesus passed His mantle (the Holy Spirit) to the disciples.
- Elisha crossed the Jordan and began his miraculous ministry with the spirit of Elijah resting on him. The disciples went out and performed the same miracles that Jesus had, with the power and person of the Holy Spirit resting on them.

The promises of God are precious. He declares something that He desires to do or give to His people. With that in mind, let us look at Romans 4:13–16.

> For the promise that he would be the heir of the world was not to Abraham or to his seed through the law, but through the righteousness of faith. For if those who are of the law are heirs, faith is made void and the promise made of no effect, because the law brings about wrath; for where there is no law there is no transgression. Therefore it is of faith that it might be according

to grace, so that *the promise* might be sure to all the seed, not only to those who are of the law, but also to those who are of the faith of Abraham, who is the father of us all. (Romans 4:13–16, emphasis added)

Justification by faith was not just for Abraham; it was for all who believed just as Abraham believed. The baptism with the Holy Spirit was not just for the disciples in the first century. It was for all who believe as they believed. These prophetic announcements pointed to a specific day. This day would change the lives of countless millions of Christians. This day was reserved for and presented to you today, a day that can change your spiritual life forever!

WHAT IS BAPTISM?

"Now John himself was clothed in camel's hair, with a leather belt around his waist; and his food was locusts and wild honey. Then Jerusalem, all Judea, and all the region around the Jordan went out to him and were baptized by him in the Jordan, confessing their sins" (Matthew 3:4–6).

Out of the wilderness came the prophet John the Baptist, dressed in camel's hair and wearing a leather belt like his predecessor, the prophet Elijah. His life and mission were formed in the wilderness with God. He was a man filled with the Holy Spirit from the womb (Luke 1:15). While his father, Zacharias, was in the temple, the angel of the Lord came down and foretold the mission of his son yet to be born:

> But the angel said to him, "Do not be afraid, Zacharias, for your prayer is heard; and your wife Elizabeth will bear you a son, and you shall call his name John. And you will have joy and gladness, and many will rejoice at his birth. For he will be great in the sight of the Lord, and shall drink neither wine nor strong drink. He will also be filled with the Holy Spirit, even

> from his mother's womb. And he will turn many of the children of Israel to the Lord their God. He will also go before Him in the spirit and power of Elijah, 'to turn the hearts of the fathers to the children,' and the disobedient to the wisdom of the just, to make ready a people prepared for the Lord." (Luke 1:13–17)

Today we put a lot of emphasis on how much "ministry" we can accomplish in our lifetimes. However, it's not how much we accomplish but whether we have done the will of Him who sent us. John's whole life was preparation for a ministry that would last a very short time! But prophets are not formed overnight, and ministers are not created in church services on Sunday. Prophets are formed in the wilderness by the Master. Their relationship with God takes precedence over everything else. The vision must be from God, not from man. The work must be of God, not of man.

Jesus said it best about His own ministry: "I have glorified You on the earth. I have finished the work which You have given Me to do" (John 17:4).

John came to announce the coming of the King and His kingdom. He came to call all to repent of their sins and to turn to this coming King for salvation. John came to prepare the way of the Lord, and water baptism prepared the people for the King. The ritual or experience of water baptism was the method of identifying all those who had come to repentance in anticipation of the coming Messiah.

Baptism means "to immerse, make fully wet, or dip." *Dipping* is a reference to the Greek process of dyeing a garment. When you are "dipped" into something, you become like it. When one is immersed in water, the water engulfs him. Water baptism was a sign of repentance. When one was baptized in water, it immediately identified them with repentance and remission of sin; and the one baptized became one with Jesus. Water baptism became what we call an *element*.

An *element* is a primary or first principle from which anything belonging to that principle has its expansion. If you associate yourself with a first principle, then you receive whatever that principle was designed to perform. So we associate John's baptism with water and repentance.

> Then Jesus came from Galilee to John at the Jordan to be baptized by him. And John tried to prevent Him, saying, "I need to be baptized by You, and are You coming to me?"
> But Jesus answered and said to him, "Permit it to be so now, for thus it is fitting for us to fulfill all righteousness." Then he allowed Him.
> When He had been baptized, Jesus came up immediately from the water; and behold, the heavens were opened to Him, and He saw the Spirit of God descending like a dove and alighting [remaining] upon Him. And suddenly a voice came from heaven, saying, "This is My beloved Son, in whom I am well pleased."
> (Matthew 3:13–17)

In other words, Jesus was saying, "It's okay, John. Leave it alone. It is fitting and proper that I do this to carry out what the Father is showing me to do, as I take my right standing in Him." Jesus did not have a sin nature like us, so this baptism was not for repentance of sin. This was a public display of His inauguration into His divine call.

When Jesus came out of the water, He saw the Holy Spirit descending upon Him like a dove. Then the Father spoke, saying, "This is My beloved Son, in whom I am well pleased." The day was coming when the Son would give up His spirit on the cross and become the sacrificial Lamb, taking away the sins of men through their confession and belief. And the dove, the Holy Spirit, would descend on all who believed in Him, just as He had descended upon Jesus.

Your confession of faith fulfills all the righteous requirements set by God. When you believe in Him, He will speak to you what He spoke to His Son: "This is my beloved son (daughter), in whom I am well pleased." Water baptism is now a symbolic act that identifies us with His death, burial, and resurrection. It is a public demonstration of an inner belief.

Another Baptism

John the Baptist announced that there were two different baptisms that believers would receive. His baptism was water baptism unto repentance. However, there was One coming after John who would baptize with the Holy Spirit and fire (Matthew 3:11; Mark 1:8; Luke 3:16; John 1:33).

Jesus made it clear to His disciples that there were two baptisms. "And being assembled together with them, He commanded them not to depart from Jerusalem but to wait for the Promise of the Father, '"which,' He said, 'you have heard from Me; for John truly baptized with water, but you shall be baptized with the Holy Spirit not many days from now'" (Acts 1:4–5).

This baptism with the Holy Spirit was a command, not a suggestion. It was not a baptism for repentance but a baptism of power, as the disciples in the upper room were all filled with the Holy Spirit with the evidence of speaking in tongues. It was very clear and evident in the first century that there were two baptisms (Acts 10, 19).

Remember the definition of baptism? It means "to make fully wet" or "to dip," like dipping a cloth into a solution of dye. Think of it this way: Water baptism is like taking a white cloth and dipping into a pitcher of clear water. The cloth goes into the water and comes out wet and is still white. The baptism of the Holy Spirit is similar, but instead of using clear water in the pitcher, we put in a red dye. The white cloth is dipped into the dye and comes out red. It is still a white cloth, but now it is directly identified with the red dye of the pitcher.

The baptism with the Holy Spirit is an immersion into the spiritual "red dye" of power. The evidence that this event has occurred is that you speak in tongues. It would be ludicrous for me to announce that I had been "water baptized" without being fully immersed in water. And I cannot announce that I am baptized with the Holy Spirit without speaking in tongues. Both water baptism and Spirit baptism are signs that an event has occurred. In the first century, in was commonplace for every believer to receive the two baptisms, and it should be that way today!

And They Were All Filled with the Holy Spirit

"And they were all filled with the Holy Spirit and began to speak with other tongues, as the Spirit gave them utterance" (Acts 2:4).

We have a lot of confusion today when we speak about the baptism with the Holy Spirit with the evidence of speaking in tongues. Most of the confusion comes from the word *baptism*. We have doctrines today that state that you are baptized with the Holy Spirit when you are saved. We have other doctrines that state that you don't receive the Holy Spirit until you speak in tongues. No wonder we have such division. Evangelicals may think Pentecostals are elitist because they claim to be "Spirit-filled." Other denominations have no idea at all that there exists in the promises of God this great experience of being baptized with the Holy Spirit with the evidence of speaking in tongues.

On the day of Pentecost, the disciples were all "filled" with the Holy Spirit. To *fill* means "to *supply* in order to accomplish." So, if you are filled with the Spirit, He is supplying you with a manifestation of His power in order to accomplish something.

This goes way beyond the word *baptism*. Jesus was filled with the Spirit after He was baptized (Luke 4:1). The baptism is the inaugural step, and the filling is the accomplishment. There are many reasons why we speak in tongues, and you will understand why we do this as you read on. Speaking in tongues is just one of several ways that the Holy Spirit "fills" us.

"And when they had prayed, the place where they were assembled together was shaken; and they were all filled with the Holy Spirit, and they spoke the word of God with boldness" (Acts 4:31).

What were they praying for? They had been threatened because they were healing the sick and preaching the Word. They prayed that God would give them more boldness in the midst of persecution. They were to be the witnesses (those willing to die for what they believed). You, as joint heirs with Jesus, can have this same boldness that the disciples received when the room shook and they received the filling to speak the Word of God with boldness.

"Now his father Zacharias was filled with the Holy Spirit, and prophesied, saying …" (Luke 1:67). Zacharias was filled with the Holy Spirit, and then he prophesied. When we prophesy, it is a result of a filling or manifestation of the Holy Spirit. He, the Spirit, supplies in order for us to do! Zacharias' wife, Elizabeth, was also filled with the Spirit and spoke over Mary. Their son, John the Baptist, was filled with the Spirit even from the womb. What did that look like?

> And it came to pass, on the next day, that their rulers, elders, and scribes, as well as Annas the high priest, Caiaphas, John, and Alexander, and as many as were of the family of the high priest, were gathered together at Jerusalem. And when they had set them in the midst, they asked, "By what power or by what name have you done this?"
>
> Then Peter, filled with the Holy Spirit, said to them, "Rulers of the people and elders of Israel: If we this day are judged for a good deed done to a helpless man, by what means he has been made well, let it be known to you all, and to all the people of Israel, that by the name of Jesus Christ of Nazareth, whom you crucified, whom God raised from the dead, by Him this man stands here before you whole. This is the 'stone which was rejected by you builders, which has become the chief cornerstone.' Nor is there salvation in any other, for there is no other name under heaven given among men by which we must be saved." (Acts 4:5–12)

The Jews wanted to know how the lame man had been healed and by what power this had been accomplished. Peter, filled with the Holy Spirit, began to preach under the inspiration of the Spirit. When I preach, I can feel the Spirit filling me with His inspiration and energy so He can say what He wants to say. Peter's mouth was moving, but it was the Spirit speaking!

> Now when they had gone through the island to Paphos, they found a certain sorcerer, a false prophet, a Jew whose name was Bar-Jesus, who was with the proconsul, Sergius Paulus, an intelligent man. This man called for Barnabas and Saul and sought to hear the word of God. But Elymas the sorcerer (for so his name is translated) withstood them, seeking to turn the proconsul away from the faith. Then Saul, who also is called Paul, *filled with the Holy Spirit,* looked intently at him and said, "O full of all deceit and all fraud, you son of the Devil, you enemy of all righteousness, will you not cease perverting the straight ways of the Lord? And now, indeed, the hand of the Lord is upon you, and you shall be blind, not seeing the sun for a time."
>
> And immediately a dark mist fell on him, and he went around seeking someone to lead him by the hand. Then the proconsul believed, when he saw what had been done, being astonished at the teaching of the Lord. (Acts 13:6–12, emphasis added)

Paul was filled with the Holy Spirit to deal with the forces of darkness as he confronted Elymas the sorcerer. We must call on the Spirit to fill us in order to cast out demons and fight the spiritual strongholds of darkness.

"And do not be drunk with wine, in which is dissipation; but be filled with the Spirit, speaking to one another in psalms and hymns and spiritual songs, singing and making melody in your heart to the Lord, giving thanks always for all things to God the Father in the name of our Lord Jesus Christ, submitting to one another in the fear of God" (Ephesians 5:18–21).

I knew what it was like to be drunk with wine, and I know what it is like to be filled with the Holy Spirit. There is no comparison between the two! When you are filled with the Spirit, you sing and make melody to worship God. You can also sing spiritual songs or sing in the Spirit in tongues. To be filled is not a onetime thing. It is designed to occur as often as needed. We must ask the Holy Ghost to fill us with all the fullness of God (Ephesians 3:19). Sometimes we do not have to ask. Sometimes He fills us full of His Spirit to accomplish His will. He supplies what we do not have.

We have learned that there are two baptisms: (1) water baptism identifies us with His death, burial, and resurrection, and (2) Spirit baptism identifies us with His power. We have also learned that the baptism with the Holy Spirit with the evidence of speaking in tongues is a filling of the Holy Spirit; one of many fillings that we can receive.

As we proceed, you will learn more about this wonderful experience of being baptized by the Holy Spirit with the evidence of speaking in tongues. It is, as I have learned in the last thirty-four years, one of the most powerful tools in the life of a Christian.

My prayer is that you receive it and use it!

THE DAY OF PENTECOST

Most of us can remember certain days that played a significant role in our lives or within the borders of our nations as they were determined by the Lord. I can remember significant events in my own life: marriage, the birth of my children, the day my first wife died, and my marriage to my second wife. I live in the United States, and Americans can remember certain significant days, such as Pearl Harbor, the assassination of President Kennedy, and 9/11. All of those days have had an influence on people in some fashion, but none of those events can be experienced again; they can only be remembered.

Christianity has two significant days that occurred in history that I have experienced over and over. They are: the death of Jesus on the cross, which brought salvation to all who believe, and the resurrection of Jesus, which ushered in the day of Pentecost and the baptism by the Holy Spirit with the evidence of speaking in tongues. This is what makes Christianity what it is. Christianity is not just history; it is a vibrant spiritual experience—one that transforms all who believe.

I believed that salvation was for me. I received all of the benefits and power proceeding forth from that decision. First, I was delivered from the power of darkness and was conveyed into the kingdom of His light (Colossians 1:13). My old life then became past tense, a history that would be obliterated by the power of grace. Second, the thirty-four years that followed have been a process of transforming me into the image of the Son (Romans 8:29). *Transformation* is a biblical word related the word *metamorphosis*: changing a caterpillar into a butterfly!

The events manifested on the day of Pentecost were for me. I received the baptism of the Holy Spirit with the evidence of speaking in tongues. Two thousand years of history did not change the promises of salvation and baptismal power. When I got baptized with the Holy Spirit, it did not become a historical, one-day event. That day birthed a power inside of me that has continued for these last thirty-four years!

Let's look at what happened on the day of Pentecost. We will deal with the prophecies pointing to this day and with the significant events surrounding Pentecost that transpired after that day in the history.

When the day of Pentecost had fully come, they were all with one accord in one place. And suddenly there came a sound from heaven, as of a rushing mighty wind, and it filled the whole house where they were sitting. Then there appeared to them divided tongues, as of fire, and one sat upon each of them. And they were all filled with the Holy Spirit and began to speak with other tongues, as the Spirit gave them utterance" (Acts 2:1–4).

What was the day of Pentecost?

Pentecost means "fiftieth." It marks the fiftieth day after Passover and is the Jewish celebration of the Feast of Weeks, commemorating the giving of the Law at Mount Sinai. Tens of thousands of people would come, some from great distances, to the temple and offer the firstfruits of their harvest.

Fifty days prior to this, another offering was made to commemorate the coming of a great harvest: the death of our Lord and the splitting of the veil in the temple, which ushered in the New Testament covenant of grace, and the ministry of the Holy Spirit that was soon to come on the earth. One was a grain offering, and the other was a blood offering.

This day of Pentecost would forever change Christianity, with the third person of the Trinity revealing Himself to govern these last days until the coming of the Lord.

There was a time marked by the Lord in eternity past when this day would come. God sits outside of what we call time. He marks and delivers events according to how He has arranged history. When He says that an event has "fully come," it means that there is no more time left before it occurs. The alarm button goes off in heaven, and the event happens!

What happened in the upper room? One hundred and twenty believers and followers of Jesus obeyed His voice and gathered in a place called the upper room to receive power. With tens of thousands of people surrounding them, they waited for the promise of the Father, the power from on high.

The only information they had was Jesus' instruction that they would receive power. I can only imagine our being there, trying to get Jesus to tell us exactly what would happen and what He meant by power.

The 120 believers in the first century were all there with one accord. All of them had committed themselves to a walk of faith, faith being the substance of things hoped for. It was a faith that didn't question God's instructions, a faith that was void of complaints. Spiritual power always flows better when there is a unity of faith. The unity of faith in Acts 2:46 produced signs, wonders, and miracles as the Lord added to the church daily those that were being saved. They were all going to be unified into one spiritual expression of power. All would be filled with the Holy Spirit and would speak in tongues as the Spirit gave them utterance. Faith can be a scary thing, because you don't get to be in control or to rest in a safe place. It is like jumping off a bridge and expecting angels to catch you every time before you hit the water.

Seed will always reproduce after its own kind (Genesis 1:12). When you plant rows of corn, you are allowing the corn to cross-pollinate, producing a more abundant crop. Do we get to pick and choose from all that Jesus and the disciples did and then decide which of those things have passed away, choosing to retain what's left so we can feel more secure and comfortable and not disturb the status quo?

In the upper room, there suddenly came a sound from heaven as a mighty rushing wind, catching them completely off guard. How did they know that the sound was coming from heaven? Wind is one of the representations of the Holy Spirit. Jesus referred to the Spirit as wind in His meeting with Nicodemus: "The wind blows where it wishes, and you hear the sound of it, but cannot tell where it comes from and where it goes. So is everyone who is born of the Spirit" (John 3:8). This strange wind began to fill and circulate through the whole house.

Then there appeared to them divided tongues as of fire. In the Greek language, it says *"like as of fire."* Another expression for *fire*, used here in the original language, is *lightning*. Lightning represents the glory or countenance of God.

"And behold, there was a great earthquake; for an angel of the Lord descended from heaven, and came and rolled back the stone from the door, and sat on it. His countenance was like lightning and his clothing as white as snow. And the guards shook for fear of him, and became like dead men" (Matthew 28:2–4).

"I lifted my eyes and looked, and behold, a certain man clothed in linen, whose waist was girded with gold of Uphaz! His body was like beryl, his face like the appearance of lightning, his eyes like torches of fire, his arms and feet like burnished bronze in color, and the sound of his words like the voice of a multitude" (Daniel 10:5–6).

The upper room was filled with the glory and presence of the living God in the likeness of the Holy Spirit. The prophecies concerning this day were at hand. Jesus, having the Spirit without measure, performing signs and wonders, was now imparting the Holy Spirit into everyone who believed.

The vision I received was what Jesus Himself had prophesied at the Feast of Tabernacles (John 7:37–39). The Spirit was not given until Jesus had been glorified. As the Lord took His rightful place back on the throne of God, the Holy Spirit rose out of Him like a golden-winged dove covered in lightning, and He fixed His piercing, fiery eyes toward the upper room. The Holy Spirit had come and was now resting on every one of the 120 believers. The implication was that every individual can receive this divine glory and presence, for God shows no partiality with His people. He gives a gift and a promise to all who believe.

So, how is this working for you so far? Imagine that you are in a prayer meeting. Suddenly you hear a mighty wind, and then 120 tongues of fire and lightning instantly appear, burning like piles of fuel, and sit on each of you. Then something begins to bubble in your abdomen, and the next thing you know, this strange language begins to come out of your mouth. Now, imagine going to your Christian friends and members of your congregation and telling them what happened. Do you want to guess at their reaction?

These 120 believers were all filled completely, supplied with the Holy Spirit, and they were the first to do an extraordinary thing: they spoke in other tongues—a divinely inspired language they had never learned—as the Holy Spirit gave them the utterance.

If you begin in the Spirit, it doesn't end! You can be filled with the Holy Spirit and speak boldly (Acts 4:31). You can be filled with the Holy Spirit and speak to one another in psalms, hymns, and spiritual songs (Ephesians 5:18–19). And you can be filled with the Holy Spirit and speak in tongues. The baptism (identification) with the Holy Spirit is a filling that produces the evidence of tongues, which completes the prophecy of Jesus that you will receive power. It isn't complicated.

In the Old Testament, Elijah's mantle of power fell upon Elisha, confirming that he was anointed to continue Elijah's ministry. The spirit of Elijah now rested on Elisha, which was evident to the company of prophets when they saw Elisha (2 Kings 2:15).

> And there were dwelling in Jerusalem Jews, devout men, from every nation under heaven. And when this sound occurred, the multitude came together, and were confused, because everyone heard them speak in his own language. Then they were all amazed and marveled, saying to one another, "Look, are not all these who speak Galileans? And how is it that we hear, each in our own language in which we were born? Parthians and Medes and Elamites, those dwelling in Mesopotamia, Judea and Cappadocia, Pontus and Asia, Phrygia and Pamphylia, Egypt and the parts of Libya adjoining Cyrene, visitors from Rome, both Jews and proselytes, Cretans and Arabs—we

> hear them speaking in our own tongues the wonderful works of God." So they were all amazed and perplexed, saying to one another, "Whatever could this mean?" Others mocking said, "They are full of new wine." (Acts 2:5–13)

Every nation under heaven was there in Jerusalem. The Tower of Babel was about to be reversed. Instead of scattering the nations, the Spirit was trying to bring them together in the unity of the Spirit. The Holy Spirit was filling His people with this new power. When people speaks in tongues, they speak a language they've never learned. Since it is a language, it will be a language originally created by God.

There are roughly 6,500 languages spoken today, and some two thousand of these are spoken by only a thousand people. There are over fifty thousand dialects to these languages, not including all the past known languages and dialects, plus the language of angels (1 Corinthians 13:1). Four reactions were distinguished when this event happened:

1. *They were confused*. Confusion causes a state of disorder. Other synonyms for the word *confused* are "disoriented, mystified, dumbfounded, and disconcerted."
2. *They were amazed*. Think of it as being out of one's mind. When a supernatural occurrence takes place in front of you for the first time, it is outside of anything your mind has recorded. You are amazed because what is taking place is amazing. Study these Scriptures regarding *amazement*: Matthew 12:23; Mark 1:27; 2:12; 6:51; 9:15; Luke 2:48; 4:36; 5:26; 9:43; Acts 3:11; 8:13; 9:21.
3. *They were perplexed*. They marveled at this event. In other words, they were experiencing what the Bible

calls a "wonder." A wonder cannot be explained, no matter what angle you observe it from or how you perceive it, based on your knowledge or ignorance of the manifestation. When you become familiar with the power of God, there are certain things that you will never be able to explain to others or yourself! You learn to accept them, becoming naturally supernatural in your walk. The word *perplexed* can also be translated as "doubt." *Doubt* is a conflict between two decisions.
4. *Others mocked*, saying, "They are full of new wine." To mock someone is to taunt, tease, ridicule, make fun of, or laugh at. These mockers were not just speaking mere words; they were laughing at the glory of God!

Not since the Tower of Babel had such a demonstration of supernatural language taken place. This event marked the birth of the New Testament church and the commencement of the last days.

The modern church, in many ways, has assumed the role of those onlookers. Many are not able to discern (distinguish) that this was a miraculous manifestation brought about by the outpouring of the Holy Spirit.

How would you respond if you heard someone say this? "Honestly, this is the truth. The other day, I saw this guy riding a mule along the side of the road. All of a sudden, the mule turned around and began to talk to him in the man's language. It was unbelievable!" (Numbers 22:22–33; 2 Peter 2:15–16).

How would you respond if you heard this? "I went camping the other day with my buddies. We were chopping up wood for a fire, and I missed the log. My axe head broke off and went flying into the water. My friend, who claimed that he was a prophet, told me not to worry. Then he just took a stick, threw it into the water, and the axe head floated to the surface of the water. It was unbelievable!" (2 Kings 6:1–7).

And how would you respond to this? "My friend John had a brother who couldn't talk. Something happened to him when he was five, and he has been that way for the last fifteen years. We heard there was a minister in our area who claimed to have the gifts of healings. We took John's brother to him for healing, and the moment his brother saw the minister, he began to convulse. The minister pointed to him and commanded a mute spirit to come out of his brother. Then immediately his brother began to talk. None of us or anyone who heard this story could remember anything like this ever happening before. It was unbelievable!" (Matthew 9:32–35).

All of these are true accounts that are recorded in the Bible. The scoffers and mockers will tell you that these things do not occur anymore. But they do occur, and they continue to happen all over the world. The lame are walking, and the blind are seeing. Demons are still being cast out of people, as the Holy Spirit continues to exercise His power through individuals. So, what do you believe?

All supernatural manifestations have one purpose. That purpose is to glorify God, not any individual, because it is God who heals people. Man is just the instrument the Holy Spirit uses to demonstrate His power and His grace. The Holy Spirit is the glory of God, and He is the Spirit of truth. When He manifests His power, it is the true power. The glory and the results will always point to Him.

If you don't understand the power of God, then why don't you ask Him about it or investigate all the wonders in the Bible? It is a much safer response than mocking something that is truly a manifestation of the glory of God.

Lisa and Gary

I first met Lisa and Gary several years ago. They were attending a church that was not receptive to the supernatural. The doctrine of the church and their denomination believed that signs and wonders had ceased at the close of the first century.

God had arranged a divine appointment for me to meet Gary. Gary began to ask me questions about the power of God. I was hesitant at first, and then the Spirit allowed me to open the floodgates of my experience and knowledge in this field. I always know when I am talking to a sponge, and Gary was soaking up everything into his spirit.

A *sponge* is my term for a person who is so hungry for the things of the Spirit that he will soak in everything you are saying, yet will confirm what you say in the Word of God. The biblical term is a *disciple*. Disciples learn to be like their teachers (Matthew 10:25).

That afternoon I met Lisa. Lisa and Gary couldn't wait to come over to my house to learn about the things of the Spirit. They also knew another couple who felt that there was more than what they were getting at church.

At my house, we began discussing the Holy Spirit, and I knew that it wouldn't be long before we talked about the baptism of the Holy Spirit with the evidence of speaking in tongues. How could I discuss the attributes of the Spirit without addressing one of His most important ones: His empowerment of our spiritual life!

I was discussing speaking in tongues, when my wife Cathy stopped me and said she needed to pray. We all prayed, and suddenly Lisa fell out of her chair onto the floor and began to speak in tongues. She couldn't speak in English, and she looked drunk. Later, I found out that she had read the related verses in Acts. She had said to the Holy Spirit that if she received this

Spirit baptism, then she wanted it just like the disciples: so full of the Spirit that they looked drunk.

Gary also received his spiritual language. One of the different kinds of tongues that came out of him was a clicking sound that flew off the roof of his mouth. For years I had taught that some languages sound really weird. One was from a tribe that communicated by making clicking sounds from the roof of the mouth. I thank God that He proved me right!

> But Peter, standing up with the eleven, raised his voice and said to them, "Men of Judea and all who dwell in Jerusalem, let this be known to you, and heed my words. For these are not drunk, as you suppose, since it is only the third hour of the day. But this is what was spoken by the prophet Joel: 'And it shall come to pass in the last days, says God, that I will pour out of My Spirit on all flesh; your sons and your daughters shall prophesy, your young men shall see visions, your old men shall dream dreams. And on My menservants and on My maidservants I will pour out My Spirit in those days; and they shall prophesy. I will show wonders in heaven above and signs in the earth beneath: Blood and fire and vapor of smoke. The sun shall be turned into darkness, and the moon into blood, before the coming of the great and awesome day of the Lord. And it shall come to pass that whoever calls on the name of the Lord shall be saved." (Acts 2:14–21)

Peter confirmed the prophecy of Joel. This was the outpouring of the Holy Spirit that would come to all flesh who believed. This was the beginning of the last days under the management of the Holy Spirit. There was still a great and terrible period to come before the coming of the Lord, and His wrath had yet to be poured out on all who reject Him. Believing produces power and glory. Unbelief produces wrath. Peter was pleading with them to turn and receive salvation.

> "Men of Israel, hear these words: Jesus of Nazareth, a Man attested [to prove, by demonstration, the existence of God and His approval of the person that is demonstrating] by God to you by miracles, wonders, and signs which God did through Him in your midst, as you yourselves also know—Him, being delivered by the determined purpose and foreknowledge of God, you have taken by lawless hands, have crucified, and put to death; whom God raised up, having loosed the pains of death, because it was not possible that He should be held by it. For David says concerning Him:
>
> 'I foresaw the Lord always before my face, for He is at my right hand, that I may not be shaken. Therefore my heart rejoiced, and my tongue was glad; moreover my flesh also will rest in hope. For You will not leave my soul in Hades, nor will You allow Your Holy One to see corruption. You have made known to me the ways of life; you will make me full of joy in Your presence.'
>
> "Men and brethren, let me speak freely to you of the patriarch David, that he is both dead and buried, and his tomb is with us to this day.

> Therefore, being a prophet, and knowing that God had sworn with an oath to him that of the fruit of his body, according to the flesh, He would raise up the Christ to sit on his throne, he, foreseeing this, spoke concerning the resurrection of the Christ, that His soul was not left in Hades, nor did His flesh see corruption. This Jesus God has raised up, of which we are all witnesses. Therefore being exalted to the right hand of God, and having received from the Father the promise of the Holy Spirit, He poured out this which you now see and hear.
>
> "For David did not ascend into the heavens, but he says himself: 'The Lord said to my Lord, "Sit at My right hand, till I make Your enemies Your footstool."'
>
> "Therefore let all the house of Israel know assuredly that God has made this Jesus, whom you crucified, both Lord and Christ." (Acts 2:22–36)

Outside of faith, what proof is there to the existence of God? When you speak to an unbeliever about Jesus, how does he or she determine that you are telling the truth? And what about the way religious people paint a portrait of our Lord? This has to go beyond human wisdom. Nicodemus discovered this when he met Jesus, realizing that no one could do the signs that Jesus did unless God was with Him. This is what *attested* means: "God is with you."

Do you realize that every time you speak in tongues you verify the existence of God? You verify that this experience, birthed two thousand years ago, is still going strong. You verify that the Lord sat down at the right hand of the Majesty on high!

Peter quoted King David as saying that death could not hold Jesus down. The one who baptized with the Holy Spirit was not left in the grave but rose from the dead. What David experienced in hope, the disciples experienced in the reality of the moment. The fullness of God through the Spirit was doing exceedingly abundantly beyond all that they could ask or think (Ephesians 3:19–21).

"And my speech and my preaching were not with persuasive words of human wisdom, but in demonstration of the Spirit and of power, that your faith should not be in the wisdom of men but in the power of God" (1 Corinthians 2:4–5).

There is more to God than just human wisdom and the preaching of His Word. There is the demonstration of His power to make it undeniably clear that He exists. Peter's message was clear to all those who ran to this manifestation of power that had invaded the natural realm for the first time since the Tower of Babel—if for no other reason than that it made those who listened without excuse.

"Now when they heard this, they were cut to the heart, and said to Peter and the rest of the apostles, 'Men and brethren, what shall we do?' Then Peter said to them, 'Repent, and let every one of you be baptized in the name of Jesus Christ for the remission of sins; and you shall receive the gift of the Holy Spirit. For the promise is to you and to your children, and to all who are afar off, as many as the Lord our God will call'" (Acts 2:37–39).

A stun gun is used to deliver electrical shock and immobilize a person. When it is said that someone is "cut to the heart," it literally means that they were "pricked in their heart." The Greek word for that is *katanusso,* which means "to stun." Not everyone there was stunned, but enough of them were shocked to the core of their inner man to ask for direction. "What shall we do?" suggests more than just a question. "What shall we do *to make a change?*" is more appropriate.

Peter told them to repent. Repentance reveals the insight of a person's mind to change the direction and purpose of his life. It is not just a command but a revelation of what is being said. Many hear, but many do not receive the revelation of what they are hearing. This message from Peter went to the core of the inner man. "Repent and be baptized in water for the remission of sin, and then you will get the second baptism: the baptism with the Holy Spirit with the evidence of speaking in tongues." Peter joined Joel, Jesus, and John the Baptist in announcing this great and wonderful gift and promise.

The Holy Spirit: The Gift Sent from God

Peter said, "You shall receive" this gift. Those words mean "to take possession of something," to take it for the rest of your life. This was not a onetime moment of ecstatic utterance. This was the beginning of a lifetime of power!

A gift is something that is freely given to you without any demands. Many times I have heard people say that they are not worthy to receive this gift or the gifts of the Holy Spirit because they are not living right. If this were the case, then none of us would be doing anything for God.

Peter realized this when he explained the healing of the man at the Gate Beautiful. "So when Peter saw it, he responded to the people: 'Men of Israel, why do you marvel at this? Or why look so intently at us, as though by our *own power* or *godliness* we had made this man walk?'" (Acts 3:12, emphasis added).

David du Plessis (pronounced "du-pley-say") was known as "Mr. Pentecost." It is said that he was the theological backbone of the Charismatic Renewal, and one of the most influential men in the twentieth century concerning the Spirit-filled life. He took this message of the Spirit-filled life to many denominations. He was, in fact, the first person I heard and saw demonstrate the power of God.

A young man approached him one day and said, "Doctor du Plessis, as a young Christian, I'm committed to serving Jesus Christ with my whole heart and to living in purity—body, soul, and mind. Still, I sometimes have struggles with my thought life. Could you tell me, sir, about how old I'll be when improper thoughts—especially about women—won't tempt my mind any longer?"

Doctor du Plessis, whose purity of life and fidelity to the truth was legendary, looked squarely into the eyes of the young man and, in the eightieth year of his own life, said, "Son, when I get that old, I'll let you know!" (Jack Hayford, *The Beauty of Spiritual Language* [Thomas Nelson, 1996], 62).

You will never be worthy enough in your own eyes to do what God has given you in the form of spiritual blessings. His death made you worthy, once and for all. You are the sons and daughters of the Most High. You are pleasing forever in His sight. It doesn't get any better than that. Your position in Him outweighs your behavior!

The Holy Spirit: The Promise Sent from God

Jesus had told the disciples to wait for the "Promise of the Father." The promise of this experience was intended for those who were at Pentecost and for those who were afar off. *Afar off* means "a great distance away." He was saying that, as many people as our God would call throughout the rest of the ages of the last days, this promise would be available to all who believed, which included you and me. Please stop telling me that certain promises have passed away. Please get your theology correct, and don't embarrass yourself with improper statements of faith that have more to do with the traditions of men than the purity of the Word!

> And with many other words he testified and exhorted them, saying, "Be saved from this perverse generation." Then those who gladly received his word were baptized; and that day about three thousand souls were added to them. And they continued steadfastly in the apostles' doctrine and fellowship, in the breaking of bread, and in prayers. Then fear came upon every soul, and many wonders and signs were done through the apostles. Now all who believed were together, and had all things in common, and sold their possessions and goods, and divided them among all, as anyone had need. So continuing daily with one accord in the temple, and breaking bread from house to house, they ate their food with gladness and simplicity of heart, praising God and having favor with all the people. And the Lord added to the church daily those who were being saved. (Acts 2:40–47)

Three thousand souls received the preaching of Peter. They got the two baptisms immediately. They were immersed in water for repentance and then filled with the living water for power. The supernatural power of God is the greatest tool for evangelism on earth. The combination of preaching and demonstration is what our Lord modeled: He preached, taught, healed the sick, cast out demons, and made disciples of men (Matthew 4:23–24).

Thousands were dispersed into many homes, being taught by the apostles as they sat around in their fellowship meals. They had all things in common. No new denominations broke the unity of the Spirit. No new traditions of men at the close of the first century said that the gifts had passed away. Everyone's needs were met. There were no theological arguments, just the simplicity of the heart, praising God and having favor with all people. God added to the church daily those who were being saved. And they were all tongue-talkers!

This is our blueprint. The ages, traditions, and systems of men have corroded the purity of this moment and movement. It can be restored, but only by the power of God. Believe with me that this blueprint will rise again from the ashes of time and take its rightful place in what we call Christianity!

TO THE ENDS OF THE EARTH

"And He said to them, 'It is not for you to know times or seasons which the Father has put in His own authority. But you shall receive power when the Holy Spirit has come upon you; and you shall be witnesses to Me in Jerusalem, and in all Judea and Samaria, and to the end of the earth" (Acts 1:7–9).

What started in Jerusalem on the day of Pentecost would later fill the whole earth. Jesus told His disciples that they would be witnesses. A witness is someone who has firsthand knowledge of a dramatic event. One who has seen or experienced an event is sometimes called an eyewitness. In the original language, a witness was also called a martyr. A martyr is one who chooses to suffer death and make great sacrifices for what he believes. The disciples, branded on the inside by this experience, were "locked and loaded."

If you talk to anyone who has experienced this wonderful baptism with the Holy Spirit with the evidence of speaking in tongues, you will soon find that they are "locked and loaded" by this experience. Now I know that "locked and loaded" is not the best theological term for this experience. But do you realize that this gift and promise is like getting a .357 Magnum gun in your spiritual holster? It's a weapon you can point directly at the Enemy and fire!

> But you shall receive power when the Holy Spirit has come upon you; and you shall be witnesses to me in Jerusalem, and in all Judea and Samaria, and to the end of the earth. (Acts 1:8)

There is a vast difference between reading Acts 1:8 in the Bible and experiencing Acts 1:8. If you read the verse you see the word *power*. But what does *power* mean if you are only reading it? If you treat it like it's any other verse in the Bible, then it is just something you read. I can study this word in the original language and realize that *power* means "might, strength, enablement, and miracles." Those too are just words. However, the words of the Bible are always pointing you to an experience.

Do you want to experience God's love or grace? Would you say that it is sufficient just to read about it in the Bible? When the word of salvation came to you, did you not take a step of faith and experience the wonders of it? So, why not believe, as we will see, that this power of Pentecost flowed to others in Jerusalem, Judea, Samaria, and the ends of the earth? The Spirit's baptism of power is still stretching out its mighty hand to take hold of you!

Acts 8

A great persecution arose in the church (Acts 8:1), and many were scattered throughout the regions of Judea and Samaria.

Sometimes the Lord uses conflict to move us to the place where He wants us. The word *scattered* means "to disperse, sow throughout, and distribute." God always knows the borders and boundaries of your existence. When these men were scattered because of persecution, they didn't go off and complain about their situations. They went and preached the Word of God everywhere. There is a lesson here for all of us to remember.

"Therefore those who were scattered went everywhere preaching the word. Then Philip went down to the city of Samaria and preached Christ to them. And the multitudes with one accord heeded the things spoken by Philip, hearing and seeing the miracles which he did. For unclean spirits, crying with a loud voice, came out of many who were possessed; and many who were paralyzed and lame were healed. And there was great joy in that city" (Acts 8:4–8).

Philip was one of the seven chosen by the apostles to watch over the widows and the poor. He was a man full of faith and full of the Holy Spirit and wisdom (Acts 6:3). Philip was called to be an evangelist, and he went to Samaria to preach Christ. All of the gifts and promises of God were now unfolding in the life of Philip. The Holy Spirit was at work, functioning in the life of this man. He performed miracles, cast out demons, and healed many who were paralyzed and lame.

Dear saint, do you understand that this is still happening today? This has happened in my own life. The Spirit's baptism is real. The gifts of the Holy Spirit are still in operation today!

> But there was a certain man called Simon, who previously practiced sorcery in the city and astonished the people of Samaria, claiming that he was someone great, to whom they all gave heed, from the least to the greatest, saying,

> "This man is the great power of God." And they heeded him because he had astonished them with his sorceries for a long time. But when they believed Philip as he preached the things concerning the kingdom of God and the name of Jesus Christ, both men and women were baptized. Then Simon himself also believed; and when he was baptized he continued with Philip, and was amazed, seeing the miracles and signs which were done. (Acts 8:9–13)

Samaria was the capital city of the northern kingdom of Israel. It was built around 800 BC by Omri, the sixth king of Israel. The Assyrians attacked it in 722 BC, and the people were carried away. The city was repopulated by people from Babylon and other places, and they brought their idol worship of demon gods with them.

Adramelech was one of the demon gods they worshipped. He was associated with Moloch. Children were sacrificed (burned) as an offering to him.

Philip entered a city where idol worship, demons, and sorcery were practiced. One can only imagine the spiritual strongholds of darkness that were ruling the lives of men. Demons are territorial. These can reside for centuries in certain regions until they are broken by the power and authority of God Himself.

Sorcery was included in the practices of magic, witchcraft, and fortune-telling. One who practices sorcery attaches himself directly to the spirits of the underworld, calling on them for power and information to control others.

Magic is a moneymaker, and Simon was celebrated for this skill. It is interesting that in Acts 8:10, he is known as "the great *power* of God." The word *power* used here is the same word and meaning that Jesus used in Acts 1:8 to describe what the disciples would receive through the baptism with the Holy Spirit. Make no mistake in thinking that demons do not have might, ability, and strength. But their strength is feeble in a confrontation with the Holy Spirit's power.

Therefore, Simon was familiar with supernatural power, but he laid it down. The preaching of Philip struck the core of his heart, and he believed and was baptized. He knew power, but when he traveled with Philip, he was amazed, in awe of the Spirit's demonstration of power. All of us would agree that we despise occult practices. Nevertheless, this historical fact tells us that the worst of them can be saved by the preaching of the Word and the demonstration of God's power.

> Now when the apostles who were at Jerusalem heard that Samaria had received the word of God, they sent Peter and John to them, who, when they had come down, prayed for them that they might receive the Holy Spirit. For as yet He had fallen upon none of them. They had only been baptized in the name of the Lord Jesus. Then they laid hands on them, and they received the Holy Spirit.
>
> And when Simon saw that through the laying on of the apostles' hands the Holy Spirit was given, he offered them money, saying, "Give me this power also, that anyone on whom I lay hands may receive the Holy Spirit."
>
> But Peter said to him, "Your money perish with you, because you thought that the gift of God could be purchased with money! You have neither part nor portion in this matter,

for your heart is not right in the sight of God. Repent therefore of this your wickedness, and pray God if perhaps the thought of your heart may be forgiven you. For I see that you are poisoned by bitterness and bound by iniquity."

Then Simon answered and said, "Pray to the Lord for me, that none of the things which you have spoken may come upon me."

So when they had testified and preached the word of the Lord, they returned to Jerusalem, preaching the gospel in many villages of the Samaritans. (Acts 8:14–26)

The events in Samaria became known to the apostles in Jerusalem. They sent Peter and John to lay hands on these Samaritans that they might receive the Holy Spirit or the Spirit's baptism with the evidence of speaking in tongues.

Peter and John were the dynamic duo that had healed the lame man at the Gate Beautiful. They were the uneducated and untrained men who had caused the religious crowd to marvel. They were men who had been with Jesus (Acts 4:13). Experiencing Jesus is a great credential for Christians. It is a demonstration of the Spirit and of power (1 Corinthians 2:4) that qualified them—and will qualify you—for ministry.

The Samaritans had only been baptized with water for salvation. Then Peter and John laid hands on them, and they received the Holy Spirit. Remember, when this passage uses the term *received*, it means that they received the same experience that the disciples received in the upper room.

The Samaritans got baptized with the Holy Spirit, and they began to speak in tongues. Simon, a man familiar with power, realized that a great power was being demonstrated. A man who is familiar with dynamite will recognize dynamite when it goes off! Simon wanted this power to do the same thing, but his heart was wrong. He saw it as a way to make money. Peter perceived this and rebuked Simon for the bitterness and sin still in his thoughts. Unfortunately, many people today abuse the power of God to make money.

Like you, I rejoice when I see someone come to the altar and receive salvation. Some people believe that we are baptized with the Holy Spirit at salvation or during some other ceremony. No one may ever convince you to change your mind, and this is not my purpose. But what was it that Simon saw that had such a profound influence on him? What caused Simon to relate it to the power that he knew? As I have said before, this experience does not make me better than you. I am better off because of the experience in my own life. I have received a power that, when confronted with demonic powers, wins every time!

Acts 9

> Then Saul, still breathing threats and murder against the disciples of the Lord, went to the high priest and asked letters from him to the synagogues of Damascus, so that if he found any who were of the Way, whether men or women, he might bring them bound to Jerusalem.
>
> As he journeyed he came near Damascus, and suddenly a light shone around him from heaven. Then he fell to the ground, and heard a voice saying to him, "Saul, Saul, why are you persecuting Me?"

And he said, "Who are You, Lord?"

Then the Lord said, "I am Jesus, whom you are persecuting. It is hard for you to kick against the goads."

So he, trembling and astonished, said, "Lord, what do You want me to do?"

Then the Lord said to him, "Arise and go into the city, and you will be told what you must do."

And the men who journeyed with him stood speechless, hearing a voice but seeing no one. Then Saul arose from the ground, and when his eyes were opened he saw no one. But they led him by the hand and brought him into Damascus. And he was three days without sight, and neither ate nor drank. (Acts 9:1–9)

The Holy Spirit has countless methods for bringing humility and repentance into your life. I had judged that a particular church I was familiar with would never see the full power of the Holy Spirit flowing in it. I was wrong! The lesson was this: Never judge, believing that a person or situation will never change—based on what you think—because you may be embarrassed by God!

I would imagine that all of us would be trapped by this statement if we had observed the life of this murderer and persecutor of Christians. It didn't seem to bother God that Saul was running around doing this. God had a plan for him, one that had been formed before the ages, and a miraculous transformation was waiting around the corner!

If a person is without hope or despairing over a loved one, he needs only to look at Paul's life, a life of power and authority rarely seen since his days as an apostle of the Lord. Salvation came to Paul, and the Spirit's baptism followed. We know, beyond a shadow of doubt, that this Spirit-filled enablement was with him: "I thank my God I speak with tongues more than you all" (1 Corinthians 14:18).

One could interpret this as a boastful statement, but this was not the case with Paul. He identified himself as the least of all the saints (Ephesians 3:8) and the least of all the apostles (1 Corinthians 15:9), so we know that it wasn't his pride making this statement.

Paul was the living, breathing example of a disciple of Christ. Whatever the Word of God had to offer in gifts and promises, he grasped them with passion. He wrote more about the power of God in the life of the believer than any other of the apostles. He gave us the revelation of the gifts of the Spirit and taught us how prophecy was to be used in the church.

Paul's preparation for ministry was simple. Wherever he went, he communicated with God through spiritual language. How else could he say, "I am glad I speak with tongues more than you all"?

"And I, brethren, when I came to you, did not come with excellence of speech or of wisdom declaring to you the testimony of God. For I determined not to know anything among you except Jesus Christ and Him crucified. I was with you in weakness, in fear, and in much trembling. And my speech and my preaching were not with persuasive words of human wisdom, but in demonstration of the Spirit and of power, that your faith should not be in the wisdom of men but in the power of God" (1 Corinthians 2:1–5).

It was Paul's demonstration of the Spirit and of power that crushed the voices of human religion, human wisdom, and human demonstration. Paul spent his life displaying and demonstrating every facet of a Spirit-filled life. It should be no different for you. What the Spirit gave to Jesus and Paul, He desires to give to you, making you more like Him and touching the lives of others!

The baptism with the Holy Spirit had been poured out on the Jews in Jerusalem on the day of Pentecost. Some ten years later, God was about to pour out His Spirit on the Gentiles. Jerusalem had a population of about forty thousand, and it increased to nearly a quarter million on the day of Pentecost. Yet God came to only 120 in the upper room. The Spirit's baptism was now going to be poured out on the Gentiles, but it would start in a home of a centurion named Cornelius.

> There was a certain man in Caesarea called Cornelius, a centurion of what was called the Italian Regiment, a devout man and one who feared God with all his household, who gave alms generously to the people, and prayed to God always. About the ninth hour of the day he saw clearly in a vision an angel of God coming in and saying to him, "Cornelius!" And when he observed him, he was afraid, and said, "What is it, lord?" So he said to him, "Your prayers and your alms have come up for a memorial before God. Now send men to Joppa, and send for Simon whose surname is Peter. He is lodging with Simon, a tanner, whose house is by the sea. He will tell you what you must do." And when the angel who spoke to him had departed, Cornelius called two of his household servants and a devout soldier from among those who waited on him continually. So when he had explained all these things to them, he sent them to Joppa. (Acts 10:1–8)

Here's what we know about Cornelius: he was a centurion, a God-fearing man, a giving man, and a man who prayed constantly.

There were three important times of prayer observed by the Jews: 9:00 a.m., 12:00 noon, and 3:00 p.m. It was the ninth hour when Jesus gave up His spirit on the cross (Mark 15:34–39), with a centurion standing next to Him and declaring that Jesus was truly the Son of God! It was the ninth hour when Peter and John encountered the lame man at the Gate Beautiful (Acts 3:1). And Cornelius had been fasting until that ninth hour when an angel of God appeared to him in a vision (Acts 10:30).

A vision is a difficult thing to explain, unless you have had one. I have seen countless visions, with my eyes open and with them shut. They can come as pictures or movies. When my eyes are shut, it is a little easier to explain. But when they are open, it is like seeing two things at once. The spiritual picture or movie comes and overlaps what you are seeing in the natural. You see? I told you it has to be experienced in order to understand it! We know that dreams and visions are part of the last days' ministry of the Holy Spirit. Much of what I speak in the prophetic is based on watching movies from heaven and then explaining what I see to the person involved.

"Confess your trespasses to one another, and pray for one another, that you may be healed. The effective, fervent prayer [to seek, ask, or entreat with an effective operating force] of a righteous man avails much. Elijah was a man with a nature like ours, and he prayed earnestly that it would not rain; and it did not rain on the land for three years and six months. And he prayed again, and the heaven gave rain, and the earth produced its fruit" (James 5:16–18).

The prayers and giving of Cornelius, like Elijah, reached God. In this case, it came as a memorial or a reminder of what was in line with God's will. His prayer was going to be answered. Your effectual prayers to receive the Spirit's baptism will be answered. Ask and you shall receive; seek and you shall find; knock and the door will be opened to you!

John Williams is considered to be one of the greatest film composers of all time, but he is no match for the "great composer" of human events on the earth. The arrangement of this spiritual score gives us a unique and fantastic perspective of how God intervenes in the affairs and directions of men.

The angel told Cornelius to send men to Joppa and gave them the GPS coordinates for Simon the tanner's house. Joppa was about thirty-six miles away, a fourteen-hour trip on foot. Meanwhile, at the sixth hour, Peter went up to the housetop of Simon the Tanner and began to pray. What a beautiful and tranquil place it must have been, overlooking the Mediterranean Sea.

While Peter was praying, he fell into a trance. A *trance* means "to throw or displace the mind out of its normal state." Other definitions include "astonished" and "amazed." Peter saw a vision in which heaven opened and an object like a great sheet, bound at the four corners, descended to the earth. In it were all kinds of four-footed animals of the earth, wild beasts, creeping things, and birds of the air. And a voice came to him that said, "Rise, Peter. Kill and eat."

But Peter said, "Not so, Lord! For I have never eaten anything common or unclean."

A voice spoke to him again a second time. "What God has cleansed, you must not call common."

This was done three times. Then the object was taken up into heaven again.

If I used the term *trance* today, many Christians would think I was deceived or under the control of Satan. Do you understand that God can throw your mind out of a normal state in order to get your attention? God knew the perfect man to answer the perfect prayer of Cornelius at the perfect time. But God had to do a work in Peter before He sent him. To Jewish thought, anything unclean could be compared to pus or leprosy. The Gentiles were also considered unclean. Peter needed a new mind-set for this new mission.

God has made some wonderful transformations in my life to prepare me for the next step. I have had to rethink a lot of traditions or "laws" handed down through the decades. Peter received a view of God's view of the Gentiles. When we receive God's view of something, it changes our view!

While Peter was thinking about this vision, the Holy Spirit told him that three men were at the front gate, seeking him. Talk about perfect timing. The Spirit told him to go, doubting nothing. "Doubting nothing" meant that Peter was to go without any discrimination. He had to walk beyond his own thought patterns. He had to walk in the Spirit and not the flesh. Seeing something you have never seen before requires a "doubting nothing" attitude.

One day, I was walking on the campus of the Bible school I attended. The Holy Spirit told me to go to the men's dorm. Those were the only directions, so I went. Then the Spirit told me to keep walking until He told me something else. As I walked through the dorm, floor by floor, I attracted a crowd. My reputation had preceded me, and the students knew I was about the Spirit's business. When I reached the top floor, God led me to a particular dorm room. I opened the door to find two roommates, who were on their knees praying. I said, "You have been asking God to give you the Spirit's baptism." They said yes, and I told them they would receive it before midnight. Before the midnight hour, both students were filled with the Holy Spirit and began to speak in tongues!

When Peter arrived at Cornelius' house, both men described the events leading to this magnificent encounter. Those in the house were ready to hear the words that God would speak through the mouth of Peter.

There is nothing that makes me more eager than to walk into an environment where the hearers are ready to hear!

Peter opened his mouth, and the first words out of his mouth were, "I perceive that God shows no partiality." Wow, talk about a new mind-set! Then he quoted one of the great passages of the Bible: "How God anointed [set apart for service and supplied the necessary power to accomplish God's purpose for our lives] Jesus of Nazareth with the Holy Spirit and with power, who went about doing good and healing all who were oppressed by the Devil, for God was with Him" (Acts 10:38).

Think of the anointing as a manifest presence of the Spirit supplying everything needed to accomplish the kingdom purpose. God was anointing the words that Peter was speaking, and then came the manifestation.

> While Peter was still speaking these words, the Holy Spirit fell upon all those who heard the word. And those of the circumcision who believed were astonished, as many as came with Peter, because the gift of the Holy Spirit had been poured out on the Gentiles also. For they heard them speak with tongues and magnify God. Then Peter answered, "Can anyone forbid water, that these should not be baptized who have received the Holy Spirit just as we have?" And he commanded them to be baptized in the

name of the Lord. Then they asked him to stay a few days. (Acts 10:44–48)

It was just like the day of Pentecost! The Holy Spirit fell on them and ignited the tongues of fire. Don't ever put God in a box. Don't ever say, "This is how God does this." Peter never gave them the ten steps to receiving the baptism with the Holy Spirit. We get so caught up in procedures that we miss the power! The hungry were ready to hear. The man was ready to preach. The Spirit was ready to act!

Acts 11

"And as I began to speak, the Holy Spirit fell upon them, as upon us at the beginning. Then I remembered the word of the Lord, how He said, 'John indeed baptized with water, but you shall be baptized with the Holy Spirit.' If therefore God gave them the same gift as He gave us when we believed on the Lord Jesus Christ, who was I that I could withstand God?" (Acts 11:15–17).

There was a time when I would have argued with Christians over doctrinal issues. However, in my latter years, I have given that up. The unity of faith of the knowledge of God may seem impossible, but God is a God of the impossible. Therefore, I will leave it to Him to convince people of their doctrines. You have every right not to believe that the baptism with the Holy Spirit and speaking tongues are one and the same experience. For me, the issue was forever settled with these verses in Acts 11:15–17.

Peter had returned to Jerusalem after the events at Cornelius' house. Then those of the circumcision, the legalists, contended with his decision to eat with the Gentiles. It reminds me of the Jews who confronted Jesus in Mark 7:1–13. Once we get set in our doctrinal ways, it is almost impossible to change our position. I am grateful to God for the subtle changes he has made over the years in me. Today, I view Christianity with a new set of eyes and a new heart. But that is a work of God, not man.

Peter recalled the events leading up to and occurring at Cornelius' house. He began in verse 15, saying, "And as I began to speak, the Holy Spirit fell upon them, as upon us at the beginning."

1. When the Holy Spirit fell on Peter at the beginning, in the upper room, they were filled with the Spirit and began to speak in tongues.
2. When Peter was speaking in Cornelius' house, the Jews with him were astonished, because the gift of the Holy Spirit was poured out on the Gentiles, and they were speaking in tongues. It verified that the same thing had happened to the Gentiles in the same way it happened to the Jews.
3. When this occurred, Peter remembered the words of the Lord spoken in Acts 1:5: "John indeed baptized with water, but you shall be baptized with the Holy Spirit."

Now, I can directly link the baptism with the Holy Spirit and speaking in tongues as one and the same event. If I sit in a crowded movie theater and yell "Fire!," I should expect people to immediately look for evidence of it, either smoke or flames. The words identify the event every time. (Conversely, if I yell

"Fire!" and there is *no* fire, especially in a movie theater, I probably will be arrested.)

When I say I was water-baptized, most people identify what I say with being submerged in water. When I say that I was baptized with the Holy Spirit, then you know I speak in tongues. That was what Peter was explaining. He directly linked the words of Jesus—"John indeed baptized with water, but you shall be baptized with the Holy Spirit"—with the event of speaking in tongues. It was not the tongues that were the primary thing. It was the power that Jesus promised with this gift: a power and authority that steadily increases over the years, a power and authority that made Paul say he was glad he spoke in tongues more than anyone!

Acts 19

Paul arrived at Ephesus on a missionary journey. It was now some twenty-five years after the events that had taken place on the day of Pentecost. The city was different, but the message was the same: "Did you receive the Holy Spirit when you believed?"

> And it happened, while Apollos was at Corinth, that Paul, having passed through the upper regions, came to Ephesus. And finding some disciples he said to them, "Did you receive the Holy Spirit when you believed?"
>
> So they said to him, "We have not so much as heard whether there is a Holy Spirit."
>
> And he said to them, "Into what then were you baptized?"

> So they said, "Into John's baptism."
> Then Paul said, "John indeed baptized with a baptism of repentance, saying to the people that they should believe on Him who would come after him, that is, on Christ Jesus."
> When they heard this, they were baptized in the name of the Lord Jesus. And when Paul had laid hands on them, the Holy Spirit came upon them, and they spoke with tongues and prophesied. Now the men were about twelve in all. (Acts 19:1–7)

Could it be, as Paul traveled through the regions, that he remembered what the Lord had said to His disciples in Mark 16?

> And He said to them, "Go into all the world and preach the gospel to every creature. He who believes and is baptized will be saved; but he who does not believe will be condemned. And these signs will follow those who believe: In My name they will cast out demons; they will speak with new tongues; they will take up serpents; and if they drink anything deadly, it will by no means hurt them; they will lay hands on the sick, and they will recover."
> So then, after the Lord had spoken to them, He was received up into heaven, and sat down at the right hand of God. And they went out and preached everywhere, the Lord working with them and confirming the word through the accompanying signs. Amen. (Mark 16:15–20)

Paul went on these missionary journeys to preach the gospel. Isn't that the Great Commission? A part of preaching the gospel, according to Jesus, is signs—like speaking in tongues, casting out demons, and healing the sick—which will be an integral part of this preaching (Mark 16:17–18).

Paul's first question to the twelve was, "Did you receive the Holy Spirit since you believed?" Their response was, "We have not so much as heard whether there is a Holy Spirit." They only knew that they had been baptized in the manner prescribed by John the Baptist, a water baptism of repentance. Paul informed them that John's baptism involved more than repentance; it required believing on Jesus and all that He had done on the cross. So that there would be no confusion—which may only be conjecture on my part—Paul gave them the opportunity to be re-baptized so that the focus would be on Jesus rather than on John the Baptist.

Paul then laid hands on them, the Holy Spirit came upon (filled) them, and they spoke in tongues and prophesied. The need implied by the question "Did you receive the Holy Spirit when you believed?" was now fulfilled.

Pauls' mission in Ephesus was not finished. It is noteworthy to examine the rest of what Paul did in Ephesus. He did what Jesus had done: preaching the gospel, teaching His words, healing the sick, casting out demons, and making disciples.

> Now God worked unusual miracles by the hands of Paul, so that even handkerchiefs or aprons were brought from his body to the sick, and the diseases left them and the evil spirits went out of them. Then some of the itinerant Jewish exorcists took it upon themselves to call the name of the Lord Jesus over those who had

evil spirits, saying, "We exorcise you by the Jesus whom Paul preaches." Also there were seven sons of Sceva, a Jewish chief priest, who did so.

And the evil spirit answered and said, "Jesus I know, and Paul I know; but who are you?"

Then the man in whom the evil spirit was leaped on them, overpowered them, and prevailed against them, so that they fled out of that house naked and wounded. This became known both to all Jews and Greeks dwelling in Ephesus; and fear fell on them all, and the name of the Lord Jesus was magnified. And many who had believed came confessing and telling their deeds. Also, many of those who had practiced magic brought their books together and burned them in the sight of all. And they counted up the value of them, and it totaled fifty thousand pieces of silver. So the word of the Lord grew mightily and prevailed. (Acts 19:11–20).

Paul spent the first three months of his time in Ephesus teaching in their synagogues. But the hearts of many began to turn against him, speaking evil of him. So Paul was able to use the facilities of the school of Tyrannus, which was named after a Greek scholar. There he withdrew with his disciples for two years, teaching and demonstrating the power of God. I heard one traveling preacher say that the effects of his teachings and demonstrations of power during that two-year period eventually produced some 320 churches and twenty-five thousand converts.

Many unusual miracles were displayed. Handkerchiefs and aprons that Paul wore were placed on the sick and those under the control of spirits, and they were miraculously healed and delivered. This was no big deal in the first century, but it is hardly believable in the twenty-first century. The teachings and demonstrations of spiritual power only highlight the struggle between the realm of darkness and the kingdom of God.

The Jewish exorcists saw the power of God at work through Paul and desired it for themselves. It is similar to that of Simon the sorcerer in Acts 8:14–25, saying, "Give me this power!" They really wanted it for their monetary gain, not to glorify God.

The exorcists made a great mistake. They assumed that by just saying the name of Jesus this spiritual power would also be theirs. The seven sons of Sceva, a Jewish priest, decided to give it a try on one who was under the control of a spirit. They said, "We exorcise you by the Jesus whom Paul preaches." The demon spirit responded by saying, "Jesus I know, and Paul I know; but who are you?" Then it jumped on them, beat them up, and sent them out of the house naked. This would have made a great video training tool for spiritual warfare.

What they didn't know was that they were working for the Devil anyway, and the Devil was not about to have his kingdom divided against itself by a few ignorant exorcists. The whole incident backfired on the kingdom of darkness. People saw and heard where the real power was coming from. It had such a profound affect that many who had practiced the occult brought their books to be burned. The Word of the Lord and the power of God prevailed (exerted or brandished power over another by means of force). In this case, the force was the enabling power of the Holy Spirit.

Jesus gave the disciples—and us—power and authority over spiritual forces of darkness. No wonder people flock to fortune-tellers and mediums. They rarely get to see the church demonstrate and prevail against these forces. "Feel good" messages do not cast out demons. Evil spirits know who has the power.

What would happen if you had to confront a demon? Would it bow to your authority or would it say, "Jesus I know, and Paul I know; but who are you?"

There was a time in my early Christian walk when sports were still a priority. Although much of that has faded, I still love to watch college basketball. Whenever I sat down to watch sports, I didn't want to be disturbed. But that was not the case on this particular Sunday afternoon.

The phone suddenly rang, and on the other end of the line was a couple in distress. Their daughter, who had always been an excellent student, was totally rebelling against them. They said that all she did now was lock herself up in her room and listen to heavy metal music. I was very familiar with the entity that was troubling her. What she didn't know was that she was surrendering her soul to evil spirits. The parents asked me if I would be willing to come to their house and talk to her. I said yes and left for their home.

When you are confronted with a situation like this, it is better not to try and figure out what the next step will be. The best advice is to pray in the Holy Spirit (in tongues), and that is what I did during the trip to their house. When I arrived, the parents told me that they had not informed their daughter that I was coming. How cute! Like I said, don't try to figure out the next step.

They got their daughter and brought her into the living room. I discerned that spirits were trying to take over her thought patterns. I began to speak to her about what was happening to her, and she stared back at me with a blank look. All of a sudden, she just got up, walked over to the chair where I was sitting, and picked up two small barbells that were next to my chair. She held them over my head and said, "I am going to kill you!"

I was not intimidated by her actions. I had perfect peace, because I knew, by faith, that I had authority over her and the spirits controlling her. I said, "No, you're not going to kill me, and I command you to put those barbells down and go back to your seat." She waited a moment and then put them down and returned to her seat. Then I took authority over those spirits and commanded them off of her. I laid hands on her, and she fell out under the power of God.

The Holy Spirit then told me that her parents needed to be baptized in the Holy Spirit with the evidence of speaking in tongues. I asked them if they wanted it, and they said yes. I laid hands on both of them, and they fell out under the power ... speaking in tongues. I just stepped over them and left, leaving all three of them on the floor under the power of the Spirit!

Sometime after that incident, they wrote me a letter and explained that their daughter had been wonderfully delivered. Her heavy metal music was gone, and she had graduated high school and was now doing very well in college.

Great and marvelous events happen through this wonderful experience of the Spirit's baptism. We have seen how three thousand souls came into the kingdom of God on the day of Pentecost. We have learned how God can deliver the worst of the occult in the stories of Simon the sorcerer and those who practiced magic in Ephesus. We have heard one of the greatest apostles of all time make it emphatically clear that he spoke in tongues more than anyone. And we have witnessed how the preaching of the gospel and leading others into the Spirit's baptism accompanied the spread of God's power from Jerusalem to Judea, Samaria, and the ends of the earth.

Now we will see the modern day explosion of this same power of the Spirit's baptism with the evidence of speaking in tongues.

THE TRADITIONS OF MEN

"There is no ignorance as dangerous as a man without any biblical experience speaking against a man with a true biblical experience."

This is the one key in this book that we want to use that *locks* a door—a door to the path of ignorance and weakness—instead of unlocking the door that gives access to our spiritual knowledge of the baptism with the Holy Spirit. This is the door that robs the body of Christ of its God-given power and puts the members of the body of Christ into bondage of law instead of grace and freedom. It is the door of the traditions of men.

These are not the traditions mentioned in 2 Thessalonians 2:15, the traditions established by word or epistle. These are the traditions mentioned by Paul in Galatians 1:14, the exceeding zeal that he'd previously had for the law and the traditions of the Pharisees. These kinds of traditions must be locked away from our bodies, souls, and spirits. This chapter provides the key to that lock.

To better understand traditions, we must examine the "laws" of tradition and how they work. Why did I pick this subject of tradition for a book on the baptism with the Holy Spirit with the evidence of speaking in tongues? Because the

Spirit's baptism represents power, and spiritual power is the one thing that makes the Devil tremble.

> Then the Pharisees and some of the scribes came together to Him, having come from Jerusalem. Now when they saw some of His disciples eat bread with defiled, that is, with unwashed hands, they found fault. For the Pharisees and all the Jews do not eat unless they wash their hands in a special way, holding the tradition of the elders. When they come from the marketplace, they do not eat unless they wash. And there are many other things which they have received and hold, like the washing of cups, pitchers, copper vessels, and couches. Then the Pharisees and scribes asked Him, "Why do your disciples not walk according to the tradition of the elders, but eat bread with unwashed hands?" (Mark 7:1–5)

The Pharisees were both a political and religious party. They believed that Jewish law had to be observed as it was written and as the scribes interpreted it. But Jewish law was more than law. Jewish law was a person's life and the way he lived it. Everything centered on it and around it.

The scribes were the ones who studied and interpreted the Mosaic laws. Their authority in interpreting the law exceeded even the law itself. Whenever Scripture is left to private interpretation, the very essence of its meaning can be changed. That change begins a new element or first principle. Once established, it becomes doctrine (rule), which passes from generation to generation.

Jewish law basically consisted of 613 commandments that could be broken down into over thirty categories. They included God, marriage, dietary rules, ritual purity, sacrifices, offerings, tithes, taxes, idolatrous practices, laws, punishment, vows, oaths, and business practices. The Shabbat, or Sabbath, had within it some thirty-nine ordinances or categories that had to be observed.

Over the centuries, the moral laws of the Ten Commandments turned into little rules and regulations, which were under the control and authority of the scribes. These regulations got passed from one generation to the next until the succeeding generations concluded that what had been transmitted to them was absolute truth—without questioning their origin or why the regulation had been enacted. They adhered to them with blind obedience.

It would take another page just to describe the method used in the washing of hands, not only before the meal but during the meal. When the Pharisees and scribes saw the disciples of Jesus eating with unwashed hands, they considered the offense profane and unclean.

The battleground was set. It would be the tradition of the elders (law and legalism) opposing the Word of God (Jesus and grace). It would be the giver of the Ten Commandments opposing the ones who had misrepresented Him. It was the Old Covenant versus the New Covenant. It was the fading glory versus the glory that excels!

> He answered and said to them, "Well did Isaiah prophesy of you hypocrites, as it is written: 'This people honors Me with their lips but their heart is far from Me. And in vain they worship Me, teaching as doctrines the commandments

> of men.' For laying aside the commandment of God, you hold the tradition of men—the washing of pitchers and cups, and many other such things you do."
>
> He said to them, "All too well you reject the commandment of God, that you may keep your tradition. For Moses said, 'Honor your father and your mother'; and, 'He who curses father or mother, let him be put to death.' But you say, 'If a man says to his father or mother, "Whatever profit you might have received from me is Corban"—' (that is, a gift to God), then you no longer let him do anything for his father or his mother, making the word of God of no effect through your tradition which you have handed down. And many such things you do."
> Mark 7:6-13

A *tradition* is something you surrender to or come under, something written or orally transmitted. *To hold* means to fiercely defend or take hold of something in order to have it as your possession.

Jesus responded to them and their doctrine. First, He called them hypocrites. A hypocrite is similar to an actor on a stage, who plays a role while wearing a mask. The essence of their pretense was their attempt to worship God through a series of rules, regulations, and traditions. But their hearts were far from Him. In modern psychological terms, they were wearing masks. Masked behavior is based on how we want to be perceived by other people, while our hearts are in a completely different place. Of course, I know that none of us would be guilty of that!

My first wife, Barbara, and I were having an argument on our way to church. Halfway there, I got a vision of opening her door, putting my foot on her side, and kicking her out at fifty miles per hour. Remember, this was a vision, but it was not from God! The heated argument continued until we arrived at the church. I got out of the car, slammed the door, and then headed for the church entrance. Then I ran into one of my Christian friends, put on a big smile, and said something like, "Well, praise God, isn't it a beautiful day?"

So many people come into a church environment wearing a mask. Why is that? Could it be because our traditions on Sunday morning might dictate that we do so? Don't our traditions cause us to do the same thing every week in the same service? Do we ever think about changing things around or giving room for the Spirit of the Lord to interrupt what we are doing?

Jesus accused the Pharisees and scribes of laying aside the commandments of God for their traditions. Not only were they laying aside the commandments of God, but they were teaching that their doctrine—beliefs that were considered authoritative and accepted—*were* the commandments of God. Why would they do that? The answer is quite simple. They were holding on to their traditions, and they were going to fiercely defend them—even against Jesus Himself! This was not only disastrous for the Pharisees and scribes, but it is disastrous for anyone who creates a doctrine or teaching outside of the Word of God.

The Pharisees and scribes had conveniently circumvented one of the Ten Commandments—the one about honoring their mothers and fathers. They had added a doctrine that allowed them to declare their money as "Corban." This term was used of goods and financial entities that had been designated as sacrifices to God or offerings toward the maintenance of the temple. The Jews to whom Jesus was speaking had concocted a scheme in which their money became an offering only to God. But their real intent was to cut off any financial aid to their parents, thus overriding one of the original Ten Commandments in the Word of God. The ultimate outcome was that the Word of God was made of no effect, removing all its power and authority, by their traditions (Mark 7:13).

During my twenty-five years of being in the organized church system, one question kept nagging me. Where had certain denominations gotten their doctrine that the baptism with the Holy Spirit with the evidence of speaking in tongues was of the Devil or mysticism, or that it was just ecstatic gibberish? And if none of those arguments worked, they simply said that it had passed away with the deaths of the original disciples—along with the gifts of the Holy Spirit and the apostles and prophets.

Here is an example of what one of the largest churches in the greater Raleigh, North Carolina, area believe about the cessation of the gifts of the Holy Spirit and ministries. This was copied from their web page: "We believe that certain gifts of the Spirit are temporary, providing the foundation for the New Testament church, and are not active today. These gifts were revelatory in nature—word of knowledge, tongues, interpretation—and were critical for a church that was without the written New Testament. Other foundational gifts were used to confirm and validate the ministry of the Apostles, such as healing, raising from the dead, as the authentic founders of the church."

This same church has a policy that if you are going to teach in their church, you are forbidden to speak in tongues, whether at the church or at home. I found that hard to believe, until I was introduced to someone who went there and confirmed it.

I do not fault them for what they believe; I just disagree with their doctrine.

Their Argument or Tradition

> Love never fails. But whether there are prophecies, they will fail; whether there are tongues, they will cease; whether there is knowledge, it will vanish away. For we know in part and we prophesy in part. But when that which is perfect has come, then that which is in part will be done away. When I was a child, I spoke as a child, I understood as a child, I thought as a child; but when I became a man, I put away childish things. For now we see in a mirror, dimly, but then face to face. Now I know in part, but then I shall know just as I also am known. And now abide faith, hope, love, these three; but the greatest of these is love. (1 Corinthians 13:8–13)

Paul was writing about the gifts of the Holy Spirit and their use in the body of Christ, both corporately and on an individual basis. First, he dealt with the gifts in 1 Corinthians 12 and then with one's use of love as it relates to the gifts in 1 Corinthians 13. Finally, in 1 Corinthians 14, he addressed the operation of the three spiritual gifts of different kinds of tongues, the interpretation of tongues, and prophecy in the corporate setting.

Beginning with 13:8, Paul mentioned that prophecy would fail, tongues would cease, and knowledge would vanish away. Paul indicated in verse 9 that we know in part and prophesy in part. Then we get to the controversial passage in verse 10: "But when that which is perfect has come, then that which is in part will be done away." Their doctrine suggests that "that which is perfect" refers to the close of the New Testament canon of Scripture, which was completed after the end of the fourth century. Another view suggests that "that which is perfect" means the second coming of Christ. So, their position is that these gifts ceased at the end of the first century. My position is that these gifts will cease when Jesus comes back at His second coming.

Now, I could argue with them against their position until Jesus comes and probably not move them in the slightest, but that is not my assignment.

Believe me when I tell you that the following is a true story.

I was taping a series on the gifts of the Holy Spirit in a studio in the Raleigh area for a television spot I had rented. I was discussing the baptism of the Holy Spirit with the evidence of speaking in tongues. I noticed that the sound engineer behind the glass was looking at me in a funny way. Then I discerned that he was a member of one of those "I don't believe that" denominations. I must confess that back in those days I was a little more contentious than I am today.

When I was through with that session, I approached him and asked him what he thought about the baptism with the Holy Ghost. I already knew the answer, but I wanted his explanation. So he immediately went to 1 Corinthians 13:8 and gave me his interpretation. I challenged him on the knowledge vanishing away. (He didn't know I was speaking about the word of knowledge.)

He had the answer, no problem. "It was the semicolons," he said. You heard me right: the semicolons! He said, "Look at these verses and notice that when it says that prophecies will fail, there is a semicolon after the word *fail*. When it talks about tongues ceasing, there is a semicolon after *cease*. But that is not the case with knowledge. There is no semicolon!"

I didn't know what to do with this theology. I desperately wanted to tell him that there was no punctuation in the original writings, but I decided to let him believe what he wanted, thanked him for his insight, and walked away.

I do not need to present a defense for something that is still in operation in the lives of hundreds of millions of born-again Christians. God is not a liar, and the Holy Spirit is not a deceiver. Would you have me believe that my best friend, the Holy Spirit, has deceived me for these last thirty-three years? I have given up trying to change the views of people or denominational doctrines. I can respect their positions, but I disagree with their interpretation of biblical theology. I am not arguing theology; I am writing about an experience. Here are a few things for you to consider concerning 1 Corinthians 13:8–13:

1. *When that which is perfect has come, then that which is in part will be done away with.* The word *perfect* means "lacking nothing necessary for completeness." That doesn't help us, because Jesus is perfect and so is the canon of Scripture. However, the use of this Greek word in the New Testament never gives any other reference to the canon of Scripture, but it does mention that our Father in heaven is perfect (Matthew 5:48).
2. *For now we see in a mirror, dimly, but then face to face.* Paul was describing what would happen when that which was perfect had come. There are fourteen references to the expression "face-to-face" in the Bible. Almost all of them deal with either a face-to-face encounter with God or with another person, not an object!

3. *Whether there are prophecies, they will fail.* To fail in the Greek language means "to be completely abolished or to render inoperative." But prophecy is flowing today through the lives of countless millions of born-again believers.
4. *Whether (if) there are tongues, they will cease.* The word *cease* in the Greek language means "to restrain a thing or a person from doing something." But millions of born-again believers are still speaking in tongues.
5. *Whether there is knowledge (or, better stated,* word *of* knowledge*), it will vanish away.* The word *vanish* in the Greek language means "to render inoperative or to put an end to something." But millions of born-again believers are still operating in spiritual revelation.
6. *Prophecy, tongues, and word of knowledge are all manifestations of the Holy Spirit.* He is the Spirit of truth. If these gifts passed away at the close of the first century, then either the Holy Spirit has also passed away or He, the Spirit of truth, is deceiving hundreds of millions of His believers. Do you really believe that?

"And it shall come to pass afterward that I will pour out My Spirit on all flesh; your sons and your daughters shall prophesy, your old men shall dream dreams, your young men shall see visions. And also on My menservants and on My maidservants I will pour out My Spirit in those days" (Joel 2:28–29).

Joel was prophesying about a time and event that would come with the outpouring of the Holy Spirit. This event occurred on the day of Pentecost in Acts 2. The disciples were filled with the Holy Spirit and began to speak in tongues. This outpouring spilled into the streets, and Peter took the occasion to relate what was prophesied by Joel. He stated the following in Acts 2:17: "And it shall come to pass in the last days, says God."

He used the expression "last days." This was the outpouring of the Holy Spirit. This was the beginning of the last days. This began the management of Christianity under the leadership of the Holy Spirit. This would last until the second coming of our Lord Jesus Christ. From the first day something is initiated until the last day designates a period of time. Therefore, it is impossible for prophecy to cease at the close of the fourth century if it is included in the last days!

Jesus was the Word of God. He stood before those Pharisees, and they argued with the very Person who had laid the foundation for them. They took what He'd started and added to it without His permission: a corrupted version of His Word. Once they'd built that ship, they were going to keep it afloat!

The Physics of an Element

"But then, indeed, when you did not know God, you served those which by nature are not gods. But now after you have known God, or rather are known by God, how is it that you turn again to the weak and beggarly elements, to which you desire again to be in bondage?" (Galatians 4:8–9). According to *Thayer's Greek Lexicon*, an *element* is "any first thing from which the others belonging to some series or composite whole take their rise; an element, first principle."

We have discussed certain key words that tell us that when a doctrine or tradition is created, it will be fiercely defended— even against the Word of God. Let's take a closer look at the word *element*. An element is a primary or first principle from which anything belonging to that principle has its expansion. If you associate yourself with any first principle, then you receive whatever that principle was designed to perform. The Pharisees, over the centuries, added many things, both oral and written, to their laws and traditions. Once these additions were in place, they were kept, and successive generations learned them and believed them to be the truth. No one questioned the validity of these new elements, because if they did, they'd get the boot. So, how did these things get added?

Galatians 4:8 tells us that when we did not know God, we served by nature (or "naturally served") other gods. Now *gods* with a small *g* is a reference to demons. Those religions that have many gods do not really have many gods; they have many *demons* disguised as God or gods. There is only one God, and anything else claiming to be a god is a demon.

Witchcraft is the exercise of any spiritual power that does not have God as its source. Paul was speaking to the Galatians, who were being bewitched by the Judaizers who wanted them to add circumcision to faith. The Judaizers were exercising witchcraft. The Devil was using them to seduce the Galatians out of freedom and into the law.

"Stand fast therefore in the liberty by which Christ has made us free, and do not be entangled again with a yoke of bondage. Indeed I, Paul, say to you that if you become circumcised, Christ will profit you nothing. And I testify again to every man who becomes circumcised that he is a debtor to keep the whole law. You have become estranged from Christ, you who attempt to be justified by law; you have fallen from grace" (Galatians 5:1–4).

The Serpent of old was trying to rob them of their freedom and power. Fallen spirits ally themselves to doctrines that countermand the spiritual laws of God.

So it is, then, in the case of the baptism with the Holy Spirit with the evidence of speaking in tongues. The issue isn't the argument between doctrinal issues held by different denominations; the issue is the attempt of the Enemy to rob Christians of the supernatural power that is their due, their inheritance. The Devil can't do anything about your salvation or where you go to church and worship. But if he can keep you from exercising the power of God against his realm of darkness, then he has won.

The apostle and the prophet represent the power of God. The nine supernatural gifts of the Holy Spirit mentioned in 1 Corinthians 12:8–10 represent the power of God. The baptism with the Holy Spirit with the evidence of speaking in tongues represents the power of God. How ironic that these are what separate true born-again believers from each other!

You have heard the expression "divide and conquer." It refers to a strategy of gaining and maintaining power, based on the fact that many smaller opponents are easier to control than one large opponent. Deception allows those with limited power (demons) to control those who would jointly have a lot more power (body of Christ). In the first century, the body of Christ was unified in its belief in the reality of spiritual power and the realms of darkness.

If you think that the author of this deception is anyone other than the Devil, then you are mistaken. I have previously stated that the one goal of the Devil is to remove the power of the Holy Spirit from the church. Just because your church preaches on the Holy Spirit does not mean that they make full application of Him. We have created the monster of denominations, which have, on occasion, established their own individual traditions above the Word. When you're in the midst of it, you become bewitched. You have no visible or viable way to comprehend what is being circulated as truth. You trust because you believe what has been handed down for generations.

I am deeply saddened when I hear denominations say that the gifts of the Holy Spirit—speaking in tongues, and the ministry gifts of apostles and prophets—have ceased. If they believe that, then they have stripped themselves of the mighty, supernatural power of God. Yes, they have the freedom to choose what they believe, but so do you!

A Sad Tale About Traditions

After I graduated from Bible school, I worked for the Federal Express Corporation as a courier. It was there that I met another courier and was able to share with him my conversion experience. Then I invited him to our church, which believed in the Spirit's baptism and the gifts. It wasn't long after that that his family came, and they all got involved with our church, receiving the power of the Spirit and all of the passion that went with it.

I moved to North Carolina, and after some time, I heard that he and his family had left the church. Evidently, he had received some teaching on the radio from a Christian whose deep-seated beliefs against tongues and the gifts had begun to sway him. Not long after that, my friend came down with a terminal illness and died. He who had once believed in divine healing had no anchor when disease struck him.

With deep sorrow, I reflected on this incident. What if our brother in Christ had been teaching on the radio that God still heals today? Isn't this the dilemma we face in Christianity? This is not the unity of faith in the knowledge of the Lord mentioned in Ephesians 4:13! My friend did have ownership of what he chose to be the truth. In either case, the good news is that he is in heaven.

> Now it happened, the day after, that He went into a city called Nain; and many of His disciples went with Him, and a large crowd. And when He came near the gate of the city, behold, a dead man was being carried out, the only son of his mother; and she was a widow. And a large crowd from the city was with her. When the Lord saw her, He had compassion on her and said to her, "Do not weep." Then He came and touched the open coffin, and those who carried him stood still. And He said, "Young man, I say to you, arise." So he who was dead sat up and began to speak. And He presented him to his mother. Then fear [which causes a person to flee or causes terror to fall upon him] came upon all, and they glorified God, saying, "A great prophet has risen up among us"; and, "God has visited His people." And this report about Him went throughout all Judea and all the surrounding region. (Luke 7:11–17)

While scanning my old Pentecostal denomination's convention website, I was looking at some of the workshops that were going to take place, and I came across this one: "How to Be Pentecostal without Killing Your Church."

The article went on to say the following: "Is it possible to present Jesus as the Baptizer with the Holy Spirit and the Healer and still grow a church in today's America? Many pastors believe in and personally practice these Pentecostal realities, but when it comes to incorporating them into the life of their congregation, they *fear* they will actually *shrink* the church rather than grow it. Images of old-time Pentecost flood their minds, and bad personal experiences make it a scary thought. The goals of this learning track will be to discuss why it's important and to suggest practical ways to minister these Pentecostal realities so that they actually help the church to grow, not become an obstacle."

Needless to say, I was greatly saddened by this concept. I read this to my wife Cathy, and she gave me some beautiful wisdom from the Lord. She said, "They are trying to manipulate their doctrine or direction instead of letting the Word of God speak for itself." So, let me break down their words and let the Word of God speak for itself.

"Is it possible to present Jesus as the Baptizer with the Holy Spirit and the Healer and still grow a church in today's America? Many pastors believe in and personally practice these Pentecostal realities, but when it comes to incorporating them into the life of their congregation they *fear* they will actually *shrink* the church rather than grow it."

Their fear is not based on the realities of the Word of God. The outpouring of the baptism with the Holy Spirit on the day of Pentecost brought three thousand converts into the kingdom of God (Acts 2:41). One of the great tools of the Enemy is to cause a spirit of fear in a pastor. Once that spirit gets its claws into the congregation, the power ceases to exist. The healing of the cripple at the Gate Beautiful led to five thousand men coming into the kingdom (Acts 4:4). This number can probably be multiplied, because the man was the head of the household and would have led other members of his family to that conclusion.

Multitudes of people came to hear Jesus because of His ability, through the Holy Spirit, to heal the sick and cast out demons (Mark 3:9–10). The word *shrink* does not appear in the Bible. Read Acts 19:1–19, and you will see how signs and wonders caused the Word of God to grow mightily and prevail over the Enemy.

"Images of old-time Pentecost flood their minds, and bad personal experiences make it a scary thought. The goals of this learning track will be to discuss why it's important and to suggest practical ways to minister these Pentecostal realities so that they actually help the church to grow, not become an obstacle."

I find it ironic that the Pentecostal denomination was founded on demonstrations of the baptism with the Holy Spirit and divine healing. Judges 2:10 says, "When all that generation had been gathered to their fathers, another generation arose after them who did not know the Lord nor the work which He had done for Israel." Could it be possible that this church had forgotten its beginnings and that another generation had grown up and completely forgotten its roots?

It is a lame excuse to state that someone else's misuses of the power of God should cause everyone to cease from signs and wonders. Would we also get rid of the pastoral ministry based on the abuses of that office in the last hundred years? The power of God is never an obstacle. It was, has, and always will be the greatest evangelistic tool in human history! Read Acts 2:41–47. Are today's pastors more afraid of offending new people coming in the door, or are they more afraid of offending the Holy Spirit?

It is always difficult to see the forest for the trees. Traditions have a subtle way of altering beliefs, and beliefs affect actions. May all of us embrace the power and splendor of the Word of God and let it speak for itself, and may we all return to our first-century roots!

"Do not quench the Spirit" (1 Thessalonians 5:19). When a fire is burning hot, one way to put it out is to throw water on it to quench it. The Spirit's baptism causes us to be filled with the Holy Spirit and fire. Fire represents presence, the presence of the Lord. We can, and do, quench His presence by our unbelief or traditions.

"Do not despise prophecies" (1 Thessalonians 5:20). Revelation 19:10 says, "And I fell at his feet to worship him. But he said to me, 'See that you do not do that! I am your fellow servant, and of your brethren who have the testimony of Jesus. Worship God! For the testimony of Jesus is the spirit of prophecy.'"

If we despise (treat as nothing) prophecy, then we will surely despise tongues and the Spirit's baptism. Imagine eliminating one avenue of communication from heaven. How this must grieve the Spirit of the Lord!

The Word of God, in many ways, becomes a choice to us. We can choose to believe everything in it as truth, or we can allow traditions to supersede the truth and make it of no effect. The choice is yours. I have made my choice. The baptism with the Holy Spirit with the evidence of speaking in tongues has richly blessed my life and the demonstration of God's power.

I loved my first church and the people in it. I am grateful to the pastor for telling me to read the Word of God and believe everything in it. And I am also grateful that certain doctrines that they kept did not take hold in my life. God loves them, and He loves me. I am not better than they are, but I am better off for what I have received.

THE BENEFITS PACKAGE

When I was in Bible school, I joined Federal Express. After they accepted me into their company, they presented me with a benefits package that included medical, dental, 401K, pension, life insurance, and few more items that I have since forgotten. I left the company in 1997, but I will still collect on the pension until I die. My wife will also collect on my pension until she dies. She is seventeen years younger than I am, so it is a great deal.

We could probably use words like *ludicrous*, *foolish*, *absurd*, and *stupid* to refer to anyone, including me, who would have turned down that benefits package and said, "No, thanks." Yet every year, I watch countless Christians turn down the benefits package of the power of God. They say "no, thanks" to the Spirit's baptism and the gifts of the Holy Spirit. They say "no, thanks" to the apostolic and prophetic ministries. But I want to talk to you who say, "Thanks, I'll take it!"

Just as there are various medical and dental benefits available, there are different benefits and uses (I call them tools) that go with this experience of the Spirit's baptism. When a carpenter builds a house, he might wear a carpenter's belt. A carpenter's belt holds a number of tools that will perform specific functions, but the overall function of the tools is to complete the design.

So it is with the baptism in the Holy Spirit with the evidence of speaking in tongues.

Some denominations make a big effort to get their parishioners to receive this experience. But rarely, if ever, have I heard anyone fully discuss all the benefits of this experience. So let me do that for you right now. Here are the benefits or tools.

Benefit #1: A Spiritual Language Flowing Out of Us

Language is an important part of our lives. It also defines our culture or nation. When we receive the Spirit's baptism with the evidence of speaking in tongues, we join the culture and nation of those who birthed this experience on the day of Pentecost. God had to specifically identify this event apart from other experiences, so He identified it through spiritual language.

The beauty of this spiritual language allowed me, for the first time in my natural life, to experience a spiritual manifestation coming forth from my spirit through my mouth (1 Corinthians 14:14). This was a critical exercise to acquaint me with the dimension of the supernatural. My natural man and mind began to learn that there was another person (spirit) inside of me that responded to the Father and had the ability to communicate with the Father. The more I do it, the more I become familiar with spiritual actions.

This later pays big dividends when we are operating within the nine supernatural gifts of the Holy Spirit (1 Corinthians 12:8–10). If you have ever studied the visions of heaven and the creatures that zoom around there, you realize that it is really weird. Well, the kingdom of God is bizarre, but it is only bizarre to humans.

One day I was at a friend's house, praying for some men. One of them fell out under the power, and his face turned bronze. It freaked his wife out and made me laugh, because I knew it was the glory of God! Jesus could have permanently turned all of us bronze to identify us with the Spirit's baptism, but He didn't. He chose a spiritual language to communicate with Him "in the Spirit."

Benefit #2: Bringing Forth Prophecy in the Corporate Setting

One of the nine gifts of the Holy Spirit mentioned in 1 Corinthians 12:8–10 is that of different kinds of tongues. When it is used, along with interpretation of those tongues, it brings forth a message from God to the people in a corporate setting for edification, exhortation, and comfort. A person must first receive the Spirit's baptism before the gift of tongues is used in the corporate setting.

Now, here is where semantics gets a little complex. When one receives the Spirit's baptism, he or she technically receives this *gift* of the Holy Spirit. "Then Peter said to them, 'Repent, and let every one of you be baptized in the name of Jesus Christ for the remission of sins; and you shall receive *the gift of the Holy Spirit*. For the promise is to you and to your children, and to all who are afar off, as many as the Lord our God will call" (Acts 2:38–39, emphasis added).

This "gift" is what we call the baptism with the Holy Spirit with the evidence of speaking in tongues. It is the *initial* evidence, and it launches one into the use of spiritual language. It is for everyone who believes, and its uses are many, as you will discover.

However, the use of this gift of speaking in tongues is limited when it is used to bring forth prophecy (tongues plus the interpretation of tongues) in a corporate setting. "But one and the same Spirit works all these things, distributing to each one individually as He wills" (1 Corinthians 12:11). As you can see, the Holy Spirit is the one who controls the use of tongues in the corporate setting, and you control its use in your own life.

Lack of understanding in the use of spiritual language produces some common errors in doctrinal thought:

1. When I am baptized with the Holy Spirit (a "day of Pentecost" experience) with the evidence of speaking in tongues, shouldn't there be an interpretation? The answer is no!
2. But wait a minute. When the disciples spilled out of the upper room, everyone in the crowd heard the disciples speak to them in their own languages. This suggests that whenever you speak in tongues, there should be an interpretation, or the words should be in the known language of the hearer, right? The answer is no!

This may sound confusing, but it really isn't. When the 120 believers received the Spirit's baptism in the upper room, they spoke in tongues, languages they'd never learned. When they came out of the upper room, they spoke the languages of all who were there, declaring the wonderful works of God (prophecy). This happened in order to prove a couple of spiritual principles:

1. Occasionally people experience the Spirit's baptism and then immediately begin to prophesy, making clear what has been spoken. Though it is unusual, it happens. God

was demonstrating, all in one moment, the two uses for the gift: being filled with power, and declaring the wonderful works of God.

2. It also disproves the cynic's view that tongues are gibberish. If tongues are gibberish, then none of those outside the upper room would have heard them speak in their own language (Acts 2:5–13). There are roughly 6,500 languages spoken today, and some two thousand of these are spoken by only a thousand people. There are over fifty thousand dialects to these languages, plus all the past known languages and dialects, as well as the language of angels (1 Corinthians 13:1). The person who calls spiritual language "gibberish" must be familiar with all of these languages and dialects to qualify that statement.

I remember a story that was told many years ago about two missionary women who had come back from China and had entered a church to seek God's direction. While they were praying, the person cleaning the sanctuary got filled with the Holy Spirit and began to praise God in tongues. What the cleaning person did not know was that he was communicating to the two women in Chinese and in the proper dialect. The Holy Spirit was using the man to tell the two women about their next assignment.

When I receive the Spirit's baptism, the evidence of that is that I speak in tongues and receive power from on high (Luke 24:49). Because I have received the Holy Spirit's baptism, He can use it to bring forth a message in a corporate setting—as long as there is an interpretation. We will get an in-depth look at this when we go through 1 Corinthians 14.

Benefit #3: Praying in the Holy Spirit for Warfare (Ephesians 6:18)

Speaking in tongues is a weapon of war. This verse in Ephesians comes at the end of the description of putting on the full armor of God so that we may be able to withstand all the fiery darts of the Enemy. There are many times when I have been in a toe-to-toe confrontation with the Enemy, and this language has become a weapon.

Benefit #4: Magnifying God (Acts 10:46) and Declaring His Wonderful Works (Acts 2:11)

My Pentecostal friends sometimes identify the Spirit's baptism as receiving one's "prayer language." That is true. However, there are times—and only you will know them—when you know that you are making declarations in the Spirit. I do not have to know what they are unless the Spirit reveals them to me, but I know that something powerful is happening in the spirit realm!

Benefit #5: Building Up Our Faith

> Now Enoch, the seventh from Adam, prophesied about these men also, saying, "Behold, the Lord comes with ten thousands of His saints, to execute judgment on all, to convict all who are ungodly among them of all their ungodly deeds which they have committed in an ungodly way, and of all the harsh things which ungodly sinners have spoken against Him."

> These are grumblers, complainers, walking according to their own lusts; and they mouth great swelling words, flattering people to gain advantage. But you, beloved, remember the words which were spoken before by the apostles of our Lord Jesus Christ: how they told you that there would be mockers in the last time who would walk according to their own ungodly lusts. These are sensual persons, who cause divisions, not having the Spirit.
>
> But you, beloved, building yourselves up on your most holy faith, praying in the Holy Spirit, keep yourselves in the love of God, looking for the mercy of our Lord Jesus Christ unto eternal life. (Jude vv. 14–21)

No one has to tell you that what Enoch prophesied is true today. The constant pounding of the world can affect your well-being. The financial market drops, the economy goes south, and you begin to fear about provision. The constant negativity produces doubt and fear.

What I am really trying to say is that there is a spiritual way to get your mind right and your faith boosted. Speaking in tongues, as stated in Jude, will build up your faith. If your muscles are weak, they do not get any stronger by just thinking about using them. Muscles work best when there is resistance. Resistance training produces greater strength.

Your natural, fleshly man is weak and needs the power of God to resist the world, the flesh, and the Devil. The more you build up your spiritual man, praying in the Holy Ghost, the more your spiritual man overrides your fleshly doubts.

Doubt (lacking faith and being conflicted between two decisions) is ugly. When your five senses drift away from the kingdom of God, there is a greater opportunity for doubt to have its way. And it is impossible to be in faith and to doubt in the same moment.

Near the end of my junior year in Bible school, my son wanted to return to our home and finish high school. The people who were renting our home were scheduled to leave at the beginning of August. I sent them a notice telling them that we would be moving back in August, and then I waited for their reply. No reply came. Finally, I called them. They had decided they wanted to stay, breaking their original agreement.

Now, what was I to do? I called my attorney, and he said it would probably take four to six months to evict them. Nothing was working, and it immobilized our whole family. All types of thoughts began to go through my head, most of them natural. Then Barbara and I began to pray in the spirit to build up our faith. When I went to bed that night, I can remember yelling the word *help* to my Father in heaven. Then the Holy Spirit spoke to me and said, "Now faith is the substance of things hoped for, the evidence of things not seen." In a split second, the gift of faith was alive in me. It was a done deal. God would fix it!

The next day was Sunday. We went to church, *believing* that God would resolve the issue. After the service, we went forward for prayer. A strong intercessor began to pray for us and said that the Lord was going to solve our problem very quickly.

On Monday morning, my lawyer called me and said that the renters had come into his office and said that they would be out of the house in four days. It was supernatural!

I have always wondered if, after we had prayed in the Spirit, the Lord might have sent Michael the archangel into their bedroom at night to make them an offer they couldn't refuse!

The Holy Spirit will *never* empower you to have doubt. However, the Holy Spirit will always react and empower the Word of God. We call it principle, and principle never operates on feelings. So, the next time you are being consumed by fear and doubt, call on the Holy Spirit to transport you to the gym of spiritual faith, where you can pump iron in the Spirit!

Benefit #6: Speaking Directly to God

"For he who speaks in a tongue does not speak to men but to God, for no one understands him; however, in the spirit he speaks mysteries [hidden things that are divinely revealed at an appointed time]" (1 Corinthians 14:2).

As I have stated before, we will eventually discuss the entire chapter of 1 Corinthians 14. For now, we are talking about a benefit for you as an individual, versus the corporate use of tongues.

There are two ways for us to verbally communicate with God. One is natural and one is spiritual. Almost all Christians take advantage of the natural communication, but many become uncertain when it comes to the spiritual. Most of our day is consumed in the natural, and that includes our language. I have found that when I am worshipping God with musical praise, my communication with Him in the Spirit increases.

Don't waste your time trying to analyze this concept. It simply says that you can speak in tongues and directly communicate with God. Well, then, what am I saying to Him when I do this? Isn't that really the question you want to ask?

Many Christians make the mistake—more often than you would think—that if they speak in tongues, they need an interpretation. That is true if you are in a corporate setting, with more than one or two others, where clarity is needed for all the hearers. You can pray that you will interpret immediately what you are communicating (1 Corinthians 14:13). However, this is not always granted by the Holy Spirit. Caution should be used when approaching interpretation. Seeking interpretation may produce *soul* interpretation, which is strictly in your own mind.

When you communicate with God in the spirit, you speak mysteries. Whenever I speak in tongues directed at the Lord, I know that there is a purposeful, spiritual communication taking place. Eventually, this communication will manifest in some form. I believe that this was one of the reasons that Paul said, "I thank my God I speak with tongues more than you all" (1 Corinthians 14:18).

No man received more revelation than Paul did. He understood what a powerful weapon he had been given by the Spirit. And it gets even better.

> However, we speak wisdom among those who are mature, yet not the wisdom of this age, nor of the rulers of this age, who are coming to nothing. But we speak the wisdom of God in a *mystery*, the hidden wisdom which God ordained before the ages for our glory, which none of the rulers of this age knew; for had they known, they would not have crucified the Lord of glory.
>
> But as it is written: "Eye has not seen, nor ear heard, nor have entered into the heart of man the things which God has prepared for those who love Him."
>
> *But God has revealed them to us through His Spirit.* For the Spirit searches all things, yes, the

deep things of God. For what man knows the things of a man except the spirit of the man which is in him? Even so no one knows the things of God except the Spirit of God. Now we have received, not the spirit of the world, but the Spirit who is from God, that we might know the things that have been freely given to us by God. (1 Corinthians 2:6–12, emphasis added)

Paul realized that his spiritual communication with God brought the necessary revelation from God at just the right time, in the right place, for the right purpose. His eyes couldn't see it, his ears had never heard it, and it was never any part of his thought process. Wow! It is the Spirit that searches the deep caverns of our souls and spirits. It is the Spirit who searches the deep things of the Father and releases the perfect communication back to us.

I love the excitement of waiting to see what the Spirit is going to release and how He will manifest it. Remember how excited you were as a child to get your hands on a box of Cracker Jacks? It was all about the toy surprise—reaching down into the box to pull it out. Spiritual communication reaches down into the wells of our inner man. The surprises that the Holy Spirit will manifest to you far exceed anything on this earth!

Don't communicate with God in this way just to get something; that is manipulation. Do it because you believe what the Word says. It is extremely rare, when the Spirit gives you a surprise revelation, that you will know that it was a result of your speaking directly to God in tongues. However, I do know that revelation and demonstration have come from this spiritual exercise of tongues.

If you are on a prayer team that prays for people, tongues will be your best friend. People often want you to agree with them about something that is based on emotion instead of sound doctrine. If you do not receive direct revelation instantly from the Spirit, then it is always a good practice to pray in the Spirit for the real answer to be given to them!

When I need my faith built up, I prepare to receive God's support when I speak in tongues. The same is true for all the benefits of spiritual action. Prepare yourself, and then descend into the depths of spiritual communication.

Benefit #7: The Spirit's Help in Our Weaknesses

"Likewise the Spirit also helps in our weaknesses. For we do not know what we should pray for as we ought, but the Spirit Himself makes intercession for us with groanings which cannot be uttered. Now He who searches the hearts knows what the mind of the Spirit is, because He makes intercession for the saints according to the will of God" (Romans 8:26–27).

Have you ever been in a rough situation? To some extent, that is a really silly question. Every Christian will face tribulation in life—something that is a burden or creates anguish, taking those who are free or unfettered and creating pressure on them. Paul, an apostle of Jesus Christ, said it this way: "Strengthening the souls of the disciples, exhorting them to continue in the faith, and saying, 'We must through many tribulations enter the kingdom of God'" (Acts 14:22). "And not only that, but we also glory in tribulations, knowing that tribulation produces perseverance; and perseverance, character; and character, hope. Now hope [a confident expectation that God will produce a favorable outcome] does not disappoint, because the love of God has been poured out in our hearts by the Holy Spirit who was given to us" (Romans 5:3–5).

Every tribulation and trial has biblical purpose. But while we are going through them, it may appear as though God has been reduced in power or has completely disappeared. God doesn't shrink or disappear. He is always the same, whether we are on the mountaintop or in the valley. He knows exactly what we are going to suffer and how that trial will eventually produce spiritual fruit. Ouch! The spiritually mature Christian knows that there is a light at the end of the tunnel. However, when we lose our spiritual insight, we only see that light as an oncoming freight train.

So He provides us, in our weak human condition, with the power of the Holy Spirit to bypass our human emotions and speak in the language of the Spirit, activating the Holy Spirit to make intercession for us. This hope of a desired outcome will never disappoint, because it is the Holy Spirit who reaches down into our hearts and pours out the love of God, giving us that confidence.

What are our weaknesses? *Thayer's Greek Lexicon* (electronic database, © 2000, 2003, 2006 by Biblesoft, Inc.) gives us a great picture of our weaknesses:

1. *Physically*, it is a weakness (infirmity) of physical health (sickness).
2. In our *souls*, it is lack of strength, which requires our mind, will, and emotions to think with a proper biblical viewpoint. It involves our inability to understand something, to do things great and glorious, or to exercise human wisdom or skill in speaking or the management of men.

3. In *warfare*, it is the inability to restrain corrupt desires and the appetite to sin.
4. In *spiritual development*, it is the inability to bear up under trials and tribulations.

Whenever we are caught in one of these conditions and do not know how to pray, then the Holy Spirit helps by going into battle for us. He, Himself, makes intercession. He approaches the King with our petitions, and the language is the language of the Spirit. The groaning, or that which cannot be uttered in human speech, is going to be in accordance with the perfect will of God.

There is never a human weakness that cannot be remedied by the power of God, but those remedies only work when they are in perfect harmony with the will of God. Jesus is the Mediator of the New Covenant (Hebrews 9:15). I believe that the Holy Spirit intercedes to the Son, who intercedes to the Father; and then the Father brings the cure. No matter how we try to explain all this, it is still a great mystery, because the Trinity is a great mystery.

Many people have come to my home, seeking healing and restoration. My preparation will always involve seeking the will of God through speaking in tongues. I never try to figure out what is going on with the person, because my human calculations are not necessarily in line with the will of God. In addition, I never allow people's emotions to affect my response. We must always allow God's wisdom to supersede our human wisdom. The prophet speaks for God, not for man!

One woman was brought to our home with a child who had a major physical defect. During my time praying in tongues, the Holy Spirit kept bringing up salvation Scriptures. When the woman came to our house, I told her that God wanted her in the kingdom of God before He would heal her child.

Now, this is not always the method that God uses to heal people, so do not accuse me of having some strange healing doctrine. Jesus was not worried about the condition of her child. He was and is well able to cause the miraculous to happen.

This woman had already committed to the Jewish faith, and she refused to seek a personal relationship with Jesus Christ when confronted. It took her only a few minutes to pack her belongings and leave the house. She wanted a quick fix from a God she did not believe in. Jesus wanted her in the eternal abode of heaven, and that was His priority. Remember that you are not here to make people feel good; you are looking for the perfect will of God in every situation.

Benefit #8: Edifying Ourselves

"He who speaks in a tongue edifies himself" (1 Corinthians 14:4).

When you exercise your spiritual language, you build up your own spiritual house. Sometimes when the battery runs down in the natural man, the battery can be charged by the spiritual man. We are living stones being built up as a spiritual house. We are a holy priesthood offering spiritual sacrifices to God (1 Peter 2:5). Therefore, when I communicate with the Lord in spiritual language, I build up my spiritual house, generating spiritual life into the dark crevasses of my soul.

Benefit #9: Worshipping God

"What is the conclusion then? I will pray with the spirit, and I will also pray with the understanding. I will *sing with the spirit,* and I will also sing with the understanding" (1 Corinthians 14:15, emphasis added).

I have been privileged to be in a congregation where the Holy Spirit has inspired, during worship, the entire congregation to sing with their spirits. It is an awesome and glorious moment—a moment soon not forgotten.

One day, I was walking by the dining hall at Bible college. There were quite a few students having fun and joking around in the entranceway to the hall. The Holy Spirit told me to go and speak to one of them. I walked up to him and said something, and the next thing I knew, all the students were down on their knees. The glory of God filled that place in a powerful way. One young woman began to sing in the spirit. I still have not heard anyone sing like that to this day. That moment started at four thirty in the afternoon and finished at twelve thirty in the morning.

This morning, I woke up and had this thought on my mind. Have you ever considered that the Lord may have created this spiritual language because He loves for us to communicate with Him in this spiritual exercise? In all that I have ever written on this subject, I have never thought about this. Maybe this gift is more for Him than for us! Now, I am not saying that this thought was from the Holy Spirit—but I'm not saying it wasn't!

All of these benefits will become perfectly clear to you once you receive this experience. In fact, it is the only way you will understand them. Your natural senses are no good in this realm. Accept by faith what the Word of God says about tongues. It is like the corporate benefits we first talked about; you have to take possession of them.

Benefit #10: Receiving Power

The last benefit listed here is the first benefit prophesied. You will receive power. You will receive might, ability, strength, and enablement to do things you couldn't do in the natural. You will receive dynamite that will be ready to explode at any moment.

1 CORINTHIANS 14

I have included 1 Corinthians 14 in this book because there has been some confusion in the church between the use of the Spirit's baptism and the gift of tongues in the church. Paul uses 1 Corinthians 14 to show the difference between the use of tongues in private and corporate situations. Hopefully, this will all be made clear by the time you have read this chapter.

"To another the working of miracles, to another prophecy, to another discerning of spirits, to another different kinds of tongues, to another the interpretation of tongues." (1 Corinthians 12:10).

The use of different kinds of tongues, interpretation of tongues, and prophecy are three gifts that have been widely misunderstood and ignored by the church at large. When one considers that Paul devoted a whole chapter of instruction for the use of these gifts (1 Corinthians 14), we should question why the use of these vocal and revelatory gifts have been neglected today. All of these gifts are a manifestation of the ministry of the Holy Spirit, and all of them greatly benefit any corporate gathering of believers (1 Corinthians 12:7).

I can still remember a particular Sunday morning service at a church I was attending. The pastor placed a microphone at the front of the church and told the congregation that if any of them had a prophetic word, they should come up front and give it. I turned to my wife and said, "You will never see anyone go up there." Why? The pastor's intent was admirable, but the congregation lacked the experience necessary to fully understand how prophecy worked. To the best of my recollection, no one ever went up.

The gift of prophecy is the ability, given by the Holy Spirit, to speak inspired utterance. The utterance is a message from God to His people in the known language of the hearers. Prophecy can also occur by means of different kinds of tongues combined with interpretation of tongues to bring a clear message. They all accomplish the same purpose: God speaks to His people.

Tongues are spiritual languages that believers receive when they are baptized with the Holy Spirit with the evidence of speaking in tongues. The first-century church received this on the day of Pentecost (Acts 2).

The baptism with the Holy Spirit, with the evidence of speaking in tongues, is a precondition for the use of the gift of tongues in a corporate setting. How could you publicly declare a message from God, in a spiritual language, unless you had first received it by means of the baptism with the Holy Spirit?

The baptism with the Holy Spirit is a gift, and the evidence that you have received it is the act of speaking in a spiritual language. The gift of tongues is also a gift, and the evidence will be a verbal expression of your spiritual language in a corporate setting. It is a spiritual communication between God and His people in a corporate gathering of two or more people. The gift of tongues acts like a verbal alarm bell, to all who are listening, that God is about to speak to them in their own language. Everyone who is baptized with the Holy Spirit receives a spiritual language unique to themselves. Therefore, the verbal declarations will be diverse. Once this gift is exercised in a corporate setting, the interpretation of tongues must follow in order to make the message clear to the hearer.

The gift of tongues *in the corporate setting* is a manifestation of the Spirit, and He prompts you to speak. When I am in private, I can initiate speaking in tongues at any time. But in the corporate setting, it is a manifestation of the Spirit, similar to a word of knowledge or any other spiritual gift.

An interpreter has the ability to translate one language into another so that the hearer has the best interpretation of what was spoken. The gift of interpretation of tongues is different from speaking in tongues. The interpreter does not understand, word for word, what was spoken in tongues. Thus, the interpretation of tongues makes clear what was spoken in tongues, but not word for word.

If a person, under the inspiration of the Holy Spirit, begins to declare a message in tongues in a corporate setting, then it must have an interpretation. Without an interpretation, there will be no clear message given to the hearer. So, let's see if this makes sense to you.

God's people gather together in a church, house, or any other congregational setting to meet and fellowship in His presence. Sometime during that gathering, the Lord purposes to speak to His people through the gifts of prophecy, different kinds of tongues, and the interpretation of tongues. He uses two avenues for this to occur in a corporate setting:

1. Prophecy: A person declares a message from God in the known language of the hearer. This can be ministered to one person or a group. Prophecy does not require an interpretation.

2. Tongues and interpretation of tongues: When it involves two people, one person gives a spiritual declaration in tongues, and then another person gives the interpretation. When it involves only one person, that one gives a declaration in tongues and then also gives the interpretation. Tongues always requires an interpretation in a corporate setting.

There has been a lot of confusion over the use of these gifts in the church. A great deal of the confusion is caused by the lack of experience and proper instruction in the church setting. We don't have to struggle or reinvent the wheel. We just need to follow the blueprints in the Bible without questioning their use!

The blueprint for using spiritual gifts is covered in 1 Corinthians 12–14. When you have a better understanding of those chapters, then you will have a greater knowledge of how all of God's gifting should be demonstrated in the church.

"Pursue love, and desire spiritual gifts, but especially that you may prophesy" (1 Corinthians 14:1). Let's look at each element of this verse.

"Pursue Love"

When I was a young boy, I loved popsicles and ice cream bars. There was an older Italian guy named Louie who drove around in a big ice cream truck and visited our neighborhood every day during the summer. When I heard the bell ring on his truck, I took off and made sure I was standing out front when he passed by. If I was late getting there, I would chase after, or *pursue*, his truck. All of the things mentioned about love in 1 Corinthians 13 must be pursued like a kid chasing after an ice cream bar.

This love is best understood when we discover how much God loves us. There is no earthly representation of that love in any human being. God's love is only an attribute of Himself. Once we discover the true nature of His love, then it transforms the way we think and act toward others.

Paul said that this kind of love could best be demonstrated in the *agape* feasts or communion. The wealthy would invite the poor to this meal, demonstrating that godly love through charity. The concept highlighted charity that was motivated not by a sense of obligation but by a genuine, Spirit-driven love.

"Desire Spiritual Gifts"

Desire is a hot, zealous passion for spiritual gifts. You want to take hold of them with the intent of never letting go. Why? Because once you have them, spiritual warfare intensifies. Why? Because the power of God distresses the realm of darkness.

It must be the zeal of God that burns in you. Not every Christian or church environment is going to welcome you or the use of these gifts. It will be the zeal of the Lord that sustains your passion when others are telling you that using these gifts is contentious and that you need to stop talking about and demonstrating them.

"But Especially That You May Prophesy"

The word *especially* means to use something more and more, to increase its quantity. One of the most desired gifts to be used in the church was prophecy. Prophecy was commonly used in the corporate setting to bring edification, exhortation, and comfort to the body. Here are some insights concerning the gift of prophecy:

- *Prophecy means speaking for God.* When the gift of prophecy is in operation, the prophetic word carries the same power and authority as if it were the audible voice of God. This becomes a holy moment and is not to be treated carelessly by either the speaker or the listener.
- *Prophecy is not by the will of man* (2 Peter 1:21). Prophecy is a divinely inspired utterance. It must never be the intent of the speaker to use this gift to bring forth his or her own will in order to manipulate others for unholy gain or control.
- *Prophecy is not for any private interpretation* (2 Peter 1:20). There is no private origin of Scripture. What the prophets spoke was not their words but the words of God inspired by the Holy Spirit. There is also no private interpretation of Scripture based on emotion or experience.
- *Prophecy is* forth-*telling.* Prophecy comes from two Greek words, *pro* (forth) and *phemi* (to speak). What you are interpreting, writing, declaring, or speaking is the will and counsel of the Lord. You are declaring something that only God knows.
- *Prophecy is* fore*telling. Foretelling* means to predict beforehand what is to come. It is comparable to Isaiah the prophet speaking the words of Isaiah 53:5, which Jesus fulfilled seven hundred years later!

"When evening had come, they brought to Him many who were demon-possessed. And He cast out the spirits with a word, and healed all who were sick, that it might be fulfilled [brought to perfect completion at the perfect time] which was spoken by Isaiah the prophet, saying: 'He Himself took our infirmities and bore our sicknesses'" (Matthew 8:16–17).

God knows the end from the beginning. He sits outside of time, but He directs the affairs of men in perfect timing. How could prophecy be true unless what was predicted came to pass every time? That was the testimony of Jesus. It was the evidence that what had been prophesied about Him had come true—and that what Jesus prophesied about the future would also come true. When Jesus tells me that He is preparing a mansion for me in heaven, I want to be absolutely sure that that I will someday be there to enjoy it!

The Sure Word of Prophecy

"And I fell at his feet to worship him. But he said to me, 'See that you do not do that! I am your fellow servant, and of your brethren who have the testimony [evidence and documentation of truth] of Jesus. Worship God! For the testimony of Jesus is the spirit of prophecy'" (Revelation 19:10).

What are the mathematical odds of Jesus fulfilling what had been spoken by Isaiah and the other prophets of old? The greatest testimony of Jesus being God is the spirit of prophecy. Many times I use the following example to show proof of the existence of God.

Professor Peter W. Stoner, who authored *Science Speaks*, stated that the probability of just eight particular prophecies being fulfilled in one person is 1 in 10^{17}, or 1 in 100,000,000,000,000,000. The eight prophecies used in the calculation were these:

1. Messiah was to be born in Bethlehem (Micah 5:2; fulfilled in Matthew 2:1–7; John 7:42; Luke 2:47).

2. Messiah was to be preceded by a messenger (Isaiah 40:3; Malachi 3:1; fulfilled in Matthew 3:1–3; 11:10; John 1:23; Luke 1:17).
3. Messiah was to enter Jerusalem on a donkey (Zechariah 9:9; fulfilled in Luke 35–37; Matthew 21:6–11).
4. Messiah was to be betrayed by a friend (Psalm 41:9; 55:12–14; fulfilled in Matthew 10:4; 26:49–50; John 13:21).
5. Messiah was to be sold for thirty pieces of silver (Zechariah 11:12; fulfilled in Matthew 26:15; 27:3).
6. The money for which Messiah was sold would be thrown "to the potter" in God's house (Zechariah 11:13; fulfilled in Matthew 27:5–7).
7. Messiah was to be silent before His accusers (Isaiah 53:7; fulfilled in Matthew 27:12).
8. Messiah was to be executed by crucifixion as a thief (Psalm 22:16; Zechariah 12:10; Isaiah 53:5,12; fulfilled in Luke 23:33; John 20:25; Matthew 27:38; Mark 15:27–28).

Stoner's statement about the mathematical probability of these eight prophecies being fulfilled in one person was validated by the American Scientific Affiliation. This number has been illustrated as follows: "If we take 1×10^{17} silver dollars and lay them on the face of Texas, they'll cover all of the state two feet deep. Now, mark one of these silver dollars and stir the whole mass thoroughly, all over the state. Blindfold a man and tell him that he can travel as far as he wishes, but he must pick up one silver dollar and say that this is the right one. What chance would he have of getting the right one?"

Professor Stoner went on to consider forty-eight prophecies. He said, "We find the chance that any one man fulfilled all forty-eight prophecies to be 1 in 10^{157}."

This is a really large number, and it represents an extremely small chance. Let us try to visualize it. The silver dollar, which we have been using, is entirely too large. We must select a smaller object. The electron is about as small an object as we know of. It is so small that it will take 2.5 times 10^{15} of them laid side by side to make a line, single file, one inch long. If we were going to count the electrons in this line one inch long, and counted 250 each minute, and if we counted day and night, it would take us 19,000,000 years to count just the one-inch line of electrons. If we had a cubic inch of these electrons and we tried to count them it would take us, counting steadily 250 each minute, 19,000,000 times 19,000,000 times 19,000,000 [nineteen million times nineteen million times nineteen million] or 6.9 times 10^{21} years. (Josh McDowell, *New Evidence That Demands A Verdict*," Nashville, Nelson, 1999, 193).

This is approximately the total number of electrons in all the mass of the known universe. In other words, the probability of Jesus Christ fulfilling forty-eight prophecies is the same as one person being able to pick out one electron out of the entire mass of our universe.

Such is the chance of any one man fulfilling any forty-eight prophecies. Yet Jesus Christ fulfilled not just forty-eight prophecies, or sixty-one prophecies, but more than 324 individual prophecies that the prophets wrote concerning the Messiah. I haven't been able to find the statistical projection representing the possibility of Jesus Christ fulfilling 324 prophecies, but I really don't think it matters, given the illustrations set forth above.

"For he who speaks in a tongue does not speak to men but to God, for no one understands him; however, in the spirit he speaks mysteries. But he who prophesies speaks edification and exhortation and comfort to men. He who speaks in a tongue edifies himself, but he who prophesies edifies the church. I wish you all spoke with tongues, but even more that you prophesied; for he who prophesies is greater than he who speaks with tongues, unless indeed he interprets, that the church may receive edification" (1 Corinthians 14:2–5).

One problem that existed in the Corinthian church was the ignorance of the believers when it came to the use of tongues. Most, if not all, had received the baptism with the Holy Spirit with the evidence of speaking in tongues, but they were deficient in differentiating between the use of tongues in their private lives and in the corporate setting.

"For he who speaks in a tongue does not speak to men but to God, for no one understands him; however, in the spirit he speaks mysteries" (1 Corinthians 14:2). Let's consider at each phrase in this verse.

- "For he who speaks": In the Greek language, this means to utter sounds without any reference to the words spoken. It is an inspirational manifestation of sound.
- "In a tongue": This refers to a language used by particular person, which distinguishes it from any other language. When the Holy Spirit gives the utterance, the person speaking speaks a language that he or she has never learned or spoken before.
- "Does not speak to men but to God": Paul was not talking about the corporate setting of believers, since no

interpretation was brought forth to make the tongues clear. He said that when we are baptized with the Holy Spirit with the evidence of speaking in tongues, we have an effective, powerful tool for spiritual growth, one that uses all the benefits of that spiritual exercise when we communicate with God.

- "For no one understands him": When I am in personal, spiritual communication with the Lord, I am using that gift for my own purpose. No one except God understands me.
- "However, in the Spirit he speaks mysteries": Mysteries are the hidden things, the secret counsel of His will (Romans 8:26–27; 1 Corinthians 2:1–13; Ephesians 6:18–19). The Holy Spirit is the one who understands what I am saying.

"But he who prophesies speaks edification and exhortation and comfort to men" (1 Corinthians 14:3).

- Edification: To *edify* is "to build up," which causes spiritual growth and development, or "to bring confirmation of something."
- Exhortation: To *exhort* means "to admonish, to appeal to one's character and conduct." Meanings for *admonish* include "to rebuke, to warn about, to give a warning, to caution, to reprove or tell off." To *discipline* and to *scourge* are also mentioned in Hebrews 12:5–6. *Exhortation* is what sports coaches do. There are times when they can be gentle, and there are times when they get right in your face and challenge you.
- Comfort: To *comfort* means "to console, soothe, or speak in a tender, intimate way to someone."

"He who speaks in a tongue edifies himself, but he who prophesies edifies the church" (1 Corinthians 14:4). Your private spiritual language edifies yourself (Jude 20), but he who speaks to the corporate body edifies the whole body. The first is internal; the second is external.

"I wish you all spoke with tongues, but even more that you prophesied; for he who prophesies is greater [better] than he who speaks with tongues, unless indeed he interprets, that the church may receive edification" (1 Corinthians 14:5).

- Paul wished that all believers would receive the Spirit's baptism. However, they were not to speak in tongues in the corporate setting without an interpretation. The problem was that many were speaking in tongues in the corporate body without interpretation.
- Paul said that prophecy is greater (better) in this corporate setting than tongues is—unless an interpretation goes with the tongues to make it equal with prophecy.
- Paul went on to say, "So that the church may receive edification." These prophetic gifts were designed to build up the church, bringing maturity and spiritual growth to the whole body. Therefore, whatever was prophesied had to be made clear to the hearers.

Why would God retract these gifts if they had such a profound benefit for his church? "But now, brethren, if I come to you speaking with tongues, what shall I profit you unless I speak to you either by revelation, by knowledge, by prophesying, or by teaching?" (1 Corinthians 14:6).

This morning I was spending some time with the Lord in worship and the reading of His Word. Then suddenly, the Holy Spirit quickened (filled) me, and off I went into tongues, praising and declaring the wonderful works of God in my spiritual language. This was the use of tongues in my private time with the Lord. I didn't receive any interpretation, but none was needed. God knew what I was declaring!

However, if this same event had occurred inside a building on Sunday morning or during any other corporate gathering, then it would have required an interpretation of my tongues so that the body of Christ might be edified by words of wisdom, words of knowledge, edification, exhortation, or prophecy in the known language of the hearer.

Now your question might be, "How do I know the difference between the private and public use of tongues when I feel this quickening to speak?" The answer is that the same Holy Spirit who quickens you in private will suddenly quicken you in public. It can be frightening to step out in faith and initiate the gift of tongues in a public setting, but you can trust Him when He prompts you.

> Even things without life, whether flute or harp, when they make a sound, unless they make a distinction in the sounds, how will it be known what is piped or played? For if the trumpet makes an uncertain sound, who will prepare for battle? So likewise you, unless you utter by the tongue words easy to understand, how will it be known what is spoken? For you will be speaking into the air. There are, it may be, so many kinds of languages in the world, and none of them is without significance. Therefore, if I do not know the meaning of the language, I shall be a foreigner to him who speaks, and he who speaks will be a foreigner to me. (1 Corinthians 14:7–11)

Musical instruments make a sound, and there is a purpose for that sound—such as a bugle or trumpet sounding the call to battle. Imagine going to hear an orchestra play but then hearing every musician play what they want without reading any music. There are specific military bugle sounds for taps, for the calling of an assembly, for charging in battle, and for retreating. Without an understanding of those distinct sounds, there would be confusion.

When I was in sixth grade, I took trumpet lessons. One of the first disciplines I learned was to play reveille. Then, at six in the morning on Christmas day, I stood in the hallway of our three-story house. With my trumpet blasting reveille, I woke up my entire family. Want to guess how it was received? I can tell you that their interpretation of my sound did not bring me comfort.

The Corinthian believers were initially going into their services and exercising their newly acquired spiritual languages without the benefit of interpretation. They, according to Paul, were literally speaking in the air. Some say that even the eldership began speaking in tongues while they were preaching—without interpretation.

There are thousands of languages, and they are all significant, but only when they are understood. Without understanding, I might as well be a foreigner in their midst. Therefore, every utterance in a spiritual tongue in a corporate gathering requires an interpretation to make clear what has been spoken in tongues.

There are, however, times when God will cause a spirit of intercession to fall on an entire congregation. Leadership may sense a moment for everyone to begin to pray in the Holy Spirit, with or without interpretation.

"Even so you, since you are zealous for spiritual gifts, let it be for the edification of the church that you seek to excel" (1 Corinthians 14:12).

What I love about this verse is Paul's positive position on Christians being zealous (passionate or in hot pursuit) of spiritual gifts. Do you think Paul would say something different to us in the twenty-first century? Yes, I know that tongues might seem like a strange manifestation to you, but it wasn't strange then; rather it was a powerful spiritual tool. The main point of Paul's message was not about tongues or spiritual gifts. The main point was about bringing the body of Christ into the proper spiritual maturity when demonstrating these gifts.

I would be the first person to tell you that there are abuses in the corporate setting when it comes to spiritual gifts. There are abuses in every corporate setting, whether the gifts are in operation or not. We are supposed to excel (abound in quantity or quality) in bringing the body into spiritual maturity.

The more the five ministry gifts—being an apostle, a prophet, an evangelist, a pastor, or a teacher—equip the saints with proper biblical conduct, the more we all share in the benefits of these gifts. You can eliminate all or part of 1 Corinthians 14, but it does not change the fact that God intended that whole chapter to be in the Bible we read in the twenty-first century. Can you even imagine God purposely confusing us when it comes to His Word?

"Therefore let him who speaks in a tongue pray that he may interpret. For if I pray in a tongue, my spirit prays, but my understanding is unfruitful" (1 Corinthians 14:13–14). When anyone exercises the gift of tongues in a public setting, that person should pray for the interpretation. This act will produce edification for the body.

Paul said that when he manifested his spiritual language, his spirit was praying, but his understanding was unfruitful or unable to do what it was created to do. In other words, his natural mind was not capable of interpreting what his spirit was speaking unless the Holy Spirit gave him the interpretation. That interpretation *could* come when he was alone, but it *must* come when he was in a public setting, either through himself or through another person manifesting the gift of interpretation.

There will be times, when you pray in tongues in private, that the Holy Spirit will immediately give you an interpretation. But let that interpretation be Spirit-driven, without trying to exert any extra effort. God is faithful. When He wants to speak to you by giving you an interpretation in private, He will do it on His terms and in His timing.

When I pray in the Spirit, I have every right to ask the Holy Spirit to give me an interpretation of my tongues. Sometimes the Holy Spirit will give me the interpretation as I am speaking in tongues. However, I always want to be careful not to allow my fleshly mind to invent an interpretation.

Now, I want to remind you again that when you pray in an unknown tongue, your spirit prays, but your understanding is unfruitful. When you receive the baptism in the Holy Spirit with the evidence of speaking in tongues, then speaking in tongues becomes a powerful weapon.

There are times when a group of intercessors will come together in prayer. They may all simultaneously pray in the spirit, and there may be no interpretation, because they are all familiar with that code of conduct. Interpretations in that setting may also be given at any time one receives the gift of interpretation of tongues. If a novice or one who is uninformed enters into the group, then they should be advised as to the nature of that intercession meeting.

"What is the conclusion then? I will pray with the spirit, and I will also pray with the understanding [mind]. I will sing with the spirit, and I will also sing with the understanding. Otherwise, if you bless with the spirit, how will he who occupies the place of the uninformed say 'Amen' at your giving of thanks, since he does not understand what you say? For you indeed give thanks well, but the other is not edified" (1 Corinthians 14:15–17).

Every believer baptized in the Holy Spirit knows that they have two different ways to communicate with God. One way is in the spirit (tongues), and the other is in the natural (their own language). The same is true for worship through song. I can sing in a spiritual or natural tongue, and the song does not have to be interpreted because it is worship to God.

"I thank my God I speak with tongues more than you all; yet in the church I would rather speak five words with my understanding, that I may teach others also, than ten thousand words in a tongue" (1 Corinthians 14:18–19).

When I read the first part of verse 18, I might assume that Paul is sounding a little arrogant. Doesn't it sound like he is boasting a little over his use of tongues? But Paul always saw himself as the least of all the saints. He was a man possessed with a spirit of humility. That humility was accompanied by tremendous spiritual power, which he received by exercising all the tools that the baptism of the Holy Spirit offered him.

Everywhere he went, he spoke in tongues. Every preparation for ministering was a spiritual preparation. Every demonic encounter was met head-on through spiritual warfare, praying in the Holy Ghost (Ephesians 6:18). Every adversity and trial meant seeking the hidden mysteries of God in the spirit (Romans 8:26). But when Paul was in the corporate or church environment, he knew that all the tongue-talking in the world would not benefit anyone else unless it was accompanied by interpretation.

"Brethren, do not be children in understanding; however, in malice be babes, but in understanding be mature. In the law it is written: 'With men of other tongues and other lips I will speak to this people; and yet, for all that, they will not hear Me,' says the Lord" (1 Corinthians 14:20–21).

Paul desired that the Corinthian church would become mature in their use of spiritual gifts. *Malice* is a desire to cause ill will or injury. The use of tongues, interpretation of tongues, prophecy, or any of the other spiritual gifts were not meant for ill will, self glory, confusion, or any other nonbiblical pattern that would create confusion or injury to others.

Paul warned the church that if they did not obey his instructions in the use of prophetic gifts, they would suffer the same consequences that Isaiah prophesied against Israel in Isaiah 28:9–13:

> "Whom will he teach knowledge? And whom will he make to understand the message? Those just weaned from milk? Those just drawn from the breasts? For precept must be upon precept, precept upon precept, line upon line, line upon line, here a little, there a little."
>
> For with stammering lips and another tongue He will speak to this people, to whom He said, "This is the rest with which you may cause the weary to rest," and, "This is the refreshing"; yet they would not hear. But the word of the Lord was to them, "Precept upon precept, precept upon precept, line upon line, line upon line, here a little, there a little," that they might go and fall backward, and be broken and snared and caught. (Isaiah 28:9–13)

Knowledge is not taught to those who are weaned from milk (babes). The Israelites did not hear and obey the words of

Isaiah, so the judgment of God fell on them by way of a foreign invader, the Assyrians, who spoke in a tongue they didn't understand. The tongues became a sign of their disobedience. This is likened to the situation in the Corinthian church, where tongues were used without interpretation. Instead of being a blessing to the congregation, it brought trouble, confusion, and disobedience, and it had the potential to produce the judgment of God.

Isaiah 28:11–12 says, "For with stammering lips and another tongue He will speak to this people, to whom He said, 'This is the rest with which you may cause the weary to rest,' and, 'This is the refreshing'; yet they would not hear." So, to the obedient came refreshing and rest, but to the disobedient came His judgment.

Let's break down 1 Corinthians 14:22–25:

> Therefore tongues are for a sign, not to those who believe but to unbelievers; but prophesying is not for unbelievers but for those who believe. Therefore if the whole church comes together in one place, and all speak with tongues, and there come in those who are uninformed or unbelievers, will they not say that you are out of your mind? But if all prophesy, and an unbeliever or an uninformed person comes in, he is convinced by all, he is convicted by all. And thus the secrets of his heart are revealed; and so, falling down on his face, he will worship God and report that God is truly among you. (1 Corinthians14:22)

Paul stated that tongues are for a sign to unbelievers. The expression "for a sign" points to something beyond itself.

It literally has to do with destination. So the believers and unbelievers were each heading for a special destination. When tongues were spoken in the corporate setting, they were pointing to the destination of interpretation.

When the believers spilled out of the upper room and spoke in tongues, the unbelievers began to mock them. But they were not mocking the believers; they were mocking the glory of God. Anytime true tongues are spoken on the earth, they are a manifestation of God's glory. Ridiculing that manifestation through unbelief will eventually produce the judgment of God.

When the Corinthian believers came together, they were speaking in tongues without interpretation. This was causing confusion, and Paul's instruction to them for proper use of the gift was a warning that if they were not obedient to the teaching, then judgment (consequences for their behavior) would also fall on them.

So, if you all come together and speak in tongues without any interpretation, will not the uninformed and unbelieving say that you are out of your mind? Of course, they will! If you have not followed the instructions for their proper use, you will see the consequences of your actions.

But if you prophesy in tongues *with* interpretation, you will bring conviction and times of refreshing, becoming mature in your understanding and following Paul's instructions—and thus producing great benefits!

"How is it then, brethren? Whenever you come together, each of you has a psalm, has a teaching, has a tongue, has a revelation, has an interpretation. Let all things be done for edification. If anyone speaks in a tongue, let there be two or at the most three, each in turn, and let one interpret. But if there is no interpreter, let him keep silent in church, and let him speak to himself and to God" (1 Corinthians 14:26–28).

Whenever the church gets together, whether in a building, home, or any other setting, it is for the edification or building up of the body of Christ. Therefore, since we have learned the value of clarity for edification, we move on to the operation of tongues in the corporate setting.

If anyone speaks in a tongue, then we will allow two or three of these declarations, each in turn, but never all of them at the same moment. There must be interpretation of each declaration, whether it comes simultaneously or spread out during the meeting. If there is no interpretation, then whoever spoke in tongues was probably manifesting his own spiritual language instead of the corporate gift. In that case, he or she should remain silent until he has matured enough in his gifting to distinguish between the two.

I remember an incident that occurred in Bible school. Every day we had chapel services, and every day at about 11:15 a.m., one student would speak aloud in tongues. However, no interpretation followed. Finally, after more than five or six days of this, I went to the dean and told him that he should resolve the error before I took action. The student was causing confusion and, with a certain degree of discerning of spirits, was operating in his flesh. This should have been addressed on the first day so that all could have learned Scriptural protocol and all could have matured.

Sometimes when a tongue is spoken, the person with the interpretation may be unaware of it or afraid to give it. This occurred at the chapel service where three hundred and fifty students attended each morning. Someone spoke in tongues, but there was no interpretation. The Holy Spirit told me the name of the person who had the interpretation. He told me that she was afraid to give it. So I yelled out, "Rita, you have the interpretation, so give it!" She straightaway gave the interpretation. I thought that was an impressive move on the part of the Holy Spirit.

There have been many occasions where a tongue was spoken in a building service, and there was no interpretation. After a few moments of silence, the pastor or one of the leaders gave the interpretation. Without being arrogant, I can tell you that my prophetic anointing discerned that most of these were not the actual interpretation, but the pastor was getting nervous because no interpretation was forthcoming. He should have used the moment to encourage a nervous interpreter or to teach on the proper procedures instead of operating in the flesh. Maybe someday pastors will finally recognize that it is always advantageous to have prophets in the building!

"Let two or three prophets speak, and let the others judge. But if anything is revealed to another who sits by, let the first keep silent. For you can all prophesy one by one, that all may learn and all may be encouraged. And the spirits of the prophets are subject to the prophets. For God is not the author of confusion but of peace, as in all the churches of the saints" (1 Corinthians 14:29–33).

In the early church, there were prophets. In some cases, there may have been two, three, or more circulating through the house churches. Why is that not the case today? When was the last time that you were in a building where there was at least one prophet, let alone two or more? This should be the model for today, for the ministry gift of the prophet is a foundational church-building gift (Ephesians 2:20).

When a recognized prophet spoke, it carried a lot of weight and authority. What they said could influence the remainder of a meeting or guide that particular body into a new direction. So, whatever was said needed to be judged to make sure that it was a true prophetic word.

The judging was done by the other prophets. If the first prophet spoke, and it wasn't a word from the Lord, then another prophet would speak. If that word was recognized by all to override the first prophet's declaration, then that first prophet was to remain silent. This was a safeguard against any type of false or immature prophetic utterances in the early church, and it should be the standard for the twenty-first-century church.

Sometimes two or three prophets might speak, and the words of their mouths herald the voice of God, and everyone knows it. In the first century, churches were houses, so one prophet might pass through, and then another, and another. They might not all be in the same house at the same time.

The spirits of the prophets are subject to the prophets. Whenever a prophet decides to speak, he is subject to:

1. The proper leading of the Holy Spirit, knowing that what he is about to speak is prophecy, or speaking for God. He is not to manipulate prophecy to get his own will or way, and he must be aware that the Enemy can trip him up. Remember that Satan spoke through Peter, and Jesus rebuked Satan.
2. Being judged by the others as a safeguard.

All of these safeguards and instructions exist to prevent confusion and disruption.

"Let your women keep silent in the churches, for they are not permitted to speak; but they are to be submissive, as the law also says. And if they want to learn something, let them ask their own husbands at home; for it is shameful for women to speak in church" (1 Corinthians 14:34–35).

This passage is one of the most misunderstood passages in the Bible. Many have woven their doctrinal statements around this passage to subvert the fullness of women as members of the same body, equal to men and entitled to exercise spiritual gifts. Yes, there are other passages where submission is the correct response, but not the way some doctrines have interpreted it.

The issue here is not that women could not prophesy, speak in tongues, give an interpretation, or operate in any other spiritual gifts. Anna (Luke 2:36) was a prophetess. Philip the evangelist had four daughters who prophesied, and the instructions for women prophesying are listed in 1 Corinthians 11:5. So the issue is not the use of prophetic gifting by women in the church.

The man was the head of the woman and the spiritual authority in the home. The woman naturally looked to the man when she didn't understand something. Considering the confusion that had already taken place over tongues, this may have been the catalyst that caused women to call out loud to their husbands, bringing on even more confusion. If the women wanted to learn something, then they were to talk to their husbands at home without disrupting the services. The church had enough problems with those who were speaking in tongues without interpretation.

"Or did the word of God come originally from you? Or was it you only that it reached? If anyone thinks himself to be a prophet or spiritual, let him acknowledge that the things which I write to you are the commandments of the Lord. But if anyone is ignorant, let him be ignorant. Therefore, brethren, desire earnestly to prophesy, and do not forbid to speak with tongues. Let all things be done decently and in order" (1 Corinthians 14:36–40).

With the repeated emphasis on proper spiritual conduct, Paul may have been dealing with many in the church who were suffering from spiritual pride. Just because the Holy Spirit manifests His presence through you, this does not give you the liberty to do what you want. Misuse of God's anointing doesn't bring about God's approval, even if it is a spiritual action.

Often, people mistakenly believe that if they prophesy, they are prophets. Prophecy is a spiritual gift given and distributed by the Holy Spirit. The ministry gift of the prophet is given by Jesus (Ephesians 4:7–11), and that gift was foreordained while the prophet was still in his or her mother's womb (Jeremiah 1:5). Prophets are not made by one's prophesying for a few minutes. Their entire lifetimes are their training field. Mature prophets may require a good twenty years of spiritual training by the Holy Spirit. Prophets prophesy, but prophesying doesn't make you a prophet.

Now, concerning the rest of you who think you are spiritual, you should heed the things that Paul has written, because they are commandments, not suggestions, from the Lord. Let the ignorant, or those who disregard and rebel against what Paul has said, remain ignorant. It is their just reward.

Therefore, in light of everything Paul said in this whole chapter, we know that he wanted believers to desire earnestly to prophesy, not to forbid the wonderful rewards that come with the baptism of the Holy Spirit with the evidence of speaking in tongues. If your building or denomination forbids this gift, then they are in violation of God's Holy Word. So, whenever these gifts manifest in church settings, let all things be done decently and in proper order.

Beware of False Prophets

I was ministering at a church in Vermont, and many signs and wonders were occurring as the Holy Spirit released the gifts of the Spirit. Near the end of my ministry time, I opened up the altar for anyone who wanted prayer for healing, and for those who had not yet received any personal ministry.

One man got up from the very back row near the front entrance. He started walking down the aisle, and the Holy Spirit gave me a discerning of spirits. The Holy Spirit told me that this man was a false prophet who was going to fake an injury so he could come up front and prophesy. It was a remarkable revelation.

When the man approached me, I asked him what was wrong. He told me that his neck hurt, but he said that he would like to say something to the congregation. Why I didn't rebuke him at that moment really puzzled me. I told him that this wasn't the time for that. I prayed for his neck, which he claimed got healed, and told him to go and sit down.

Then the Holy Spirit led me toward a woman in the congregation. I was halfway down the aisle when that false prophet got up to prophesy. So evil were his ways that he was going to fake tongues and an interpretation in order to spill his venom. The Holy Spirit, in the form of the Lion of the tribe of Judah, came roaring out of me! With a fury birthed within the wells of my spirit, these words came forth: "Sit down and shut up!" It felt like the whole building shook with the wrath of God.

The man immediately shut up, while the entire congregation looked like they had just seen King Kong enter the building. Then I commanded him to leave the building and never return—or I would personally throw him out. He left before I could take a chunk out of his hide. There was no time for civility or permission from the pastor. This was war!

The congregation was stunned. Many of them had anger on their faces, and it was directed at me. So I took the opportunity to teach about false prophets and to explain how the Holy Spirit had led me. Then a woman raised her hand and confirmed that this man had been going around to all the churches in the area and prophesying things that were not from God. He truly was a false prophet. I was grateful for the woman's testimony, and I hoped that the congregation was grateful to the Holy Spirit for teaching them about the discerning of spirits.

Why didn't I cast the spirit off of him? Well, for one reason, I was not led by the Holy Spirit to do that. But I also speculated that this man had been given over to evil spirits because of his rebellion and unwillingness to submit to correction.

There is a metaphor that fits this occasion. If you place a frog in boiling water, he will immediately jump out. But if you place the frog in cold water, and slowly turn up the heat, he will eventually be boiled to death. I had always thought this to be true, until I read that studies at Harvard University in 1995 had proved this to be false. Nevertheless, the frog in cold water represents the world and unbelieving Christians who are unaware that spirits are constantly trying to deceive and subject them to their control by slowly turning up the heat.

God desires that the body of Christ operate in prophetic gifting. God has always placed teachers of these gifts in the body. God is not afraid of false prophets, and neither should any believer be. The prophetic gifts edify, exhort, and comfort the body of Christ. We must pray and ask the Lord to grow us all in the mature use of these gifts! Maturity brings understanding, understanding brings proper use, and proper use will quench all the fiery darts of the Enemy!

THE MODERN DAY EXPLOSION

"Revival affects those experiencing it—not those who observe it!" (author unknown).

> Now when these things had been thus prepared, the priests always went into the first part of the tabernacle, performing the services. But into the second part the high priest went alone once a year, not without blood, which he offered for himself and for the people's sins committed in ignorance; the Holy Spirit indicating this, that the way into the Holiest of All was not yet made manifest while the first tabernacle was still standing. It was symbolic for the present time in which both gifts and sacrifices are offered which cannot make him who performed the service perfect in regard to the conscience—concerned only with foods and drinks, various washings, and fleshly ordinances imposed until the time of reformation [to correct, make

improvements, or thoroughly straighten out].
(Hebrews 9:6–10)

I am not a huge advocate of the word *revival*. I believe it does have a place in Christianity if we see it as something that restores one to spiritual life or awakens a movement that has been dormant for years. In the modern era we live in, that word has been diluted through the media of Christian advertising. Churches announce revivals in advance: "Come and join us in two weeks for Holy Ghost revival!" Unfortunately, many of those meetings do just the opposite of bringing people back to life. I believe that any great move of God, or revival, directly links us to the one and only reformation in history.

You are probably thinking of the Protestant Reformation in the sixteenth century, but I am not. Yes, the Protestant Reformation did bring many out of the slavery of religious doctrine through the concept of justification by faith through the teachings of men like Luther and Calvin. But it did very little to link us to what I consider the only real reformation in history: the veil splitting in the temple, giving us direct access to God's glory because of Christ's death on the cross.

That moment forever changed the way God deals with His people. That moment ended the old covenant (testament) of law, and ushered in the new covenant of grace and justification by faith. It gave every believer access to the throne of God and released the Holy Spirit to administer and manage the last days of human history. Although the Protestant Reformation restored the teachings of grace and justification to a legalistic church system, it never solved the issues of the fivefold ministry of the apostle, prophet, evangelist, pastor, and teacher. It never released the fullness of the gifts of the Holy Spirit that were such an integral part of a believer's life.

The first-century reformation gave us a blueprint for all time.

> And they continued steadfastly in the apostles' doctrine and fellowship, in the breaking of bread, and in prayers. Then fear came upon every soul, and many wonders and signs were done through the apostles. Now all who believed were together, and had all things in common, and sold their possessions and goods, and divided them among all, as anyone had need. So continuing daily with one accord in the temple, and breaking bread from house to house, they ate their food with gladness and simplicity of heart, praising God and having favor with all the people. And the Lord added to the church daily those who were being saved. (Acts 2:42–47)

From the days of John the Baptist to the apostle John's writing of the book of Revelation, we have a sixty-year blueprint of Christianity, a blueprint that has not been duplicated for two thousand years. Our modern system of "church" was not in its embryonic stage until three hundred years after the close of the first century. How would our first-century forefathers view our current system if they were to compare what they did to what we do?

Manifestations of the Holy Spirit's power through healing and deliverance disappeared within the first one hundred years after the close of the first century. The gifts of the Holy Spirit and the Spirit's baptism were still functioning throughout the intervening centuries, but in the last three hundred years, there has been a worldwide outpouring of the Spirit that has easily overshadowed the previous 1,700 years.

Therefore, when I think of revival, I think of God's reformation of the church. I think in terms what took place in the first century. I look at the original blueprint and compare it to today.

I think of the ministry of Jesus.

> And Jesus went about all Galilee, teaching in their synagogues, preaching the gospel of the kingdom, and healing all kinds of sickness and all kinds of disease among the people. Then His fame went throughout all Syria; and they brought to Him all sick people who were afflicted with various diseases and torments, and those who were demon-possessed, epileptics, and paralytics; and He healed them. Great multitudes followed Him—from Galilee, and from Decapolis, Jerusalem, Judea, and beyond the Jordan" (Matthew 4:23–25).

I think of the ministry of the disciples.

> Then He called His twelve disciples together and gave them power and authority over all demons, and to cure diseases. He sent them to preach the kingdom of God and to heal the sick. And He said to them, "Take nothing for the journey, neither staffs nor bag nor bread nor money; and do not have two tunics apiece. Whatever house you enter, stay there, and from there depart.

> And whoever will not receive you, when you go out of that city, shake off the very dust from your feet as a testimony against them." So they departed and went through the towns, preaching the gospel and healing everywhere. (Luke 9:1–6)

I think of the five ministry gifts.

> And He Himself gave some to be apostles, some prophets, some evangelists, and some pastors and teachers, for the equipping of the saints for the work of ministry, for the edifying of the body of Christ, till we all come to the unity of the faith and of the knowledge of the Son of God, to a perfect man, to the measure of the stature of the fullness of Christ; that we should no longer be children, tossed to and fro and carried about with every wind of doctrine, by the trickery of men, in the cunning craftiness of deceitful plotting, but, speaking the truth in love, may grow up in all things into Him who is the head—Christ—from whom the whole body, joined and knit together by what every joint supplies, according to the effective working by which every part does its share, causes growth of the body for the edifying of itself in love. (Ephesians 4:11–16)

And I think of the ministry of the Holy Spirit.

> And He said to them, "It is not for you to know times or seasons which the Father has put in

> His own authority. But you shall receive power when the Holy Spirit has come upon you; and you shall be witnesses to Me in Jerusalem, and in all Judea and Samaria, and to the end of the earth." (Acts 1:7–8)

When I see the events depicted in these Scriptures occurring today, then I know that I am directly linked to the reformation of the first century. Maybe I am a dreamer and not grounded in reality. Since the day that the Spirit's baptism came into my life, I have thought only about what it would be like to have lived in that time. I have experienced all the manifestations of the Spirit that they experienced. I have experienced the training of God, the Holy Spirit, and becoming one of His prophetic servants. And I have experienced "church," both in a building on Sunday and in houses, restaurants, and any other place were believers gather together on any day of the week to talk about God.

I have also experienced the aggregate of two thousand years of the traditions of men and denominational doctrines. Some are good. Some are bad. And some are good and bad. The traditions of men have hindered the purity of a true reformation.

Am I looking for perfection? Of course not! Our natures are no different from those of the Israelites—except that we live in a better covenant or agreement with God. We are fallen creatures that God loves, no matter how we behave or how we mess up "church."

In spite of all our imperfections, the kingdom of God is still on the move. My heart has always gone out to those in the kingdom who have missed out on the power and deliverance portions of Jesus' ministry. My calling has always been, and will always be, to bring that power to as many as will receive it.

The Azusa Street Revival

The Azusa Street Revival was the gateway for the twentieth-century outpouring of the Holy Spirit.

"And He said, 'The kingdom of God is as if a man should scatter seed on the ground, and should sleep by night and rise by day, and the seed should sprout and grow, he himself does not know how. For the earth yields crops by itself: first the blade, then the head, after that the full grain in the head. But when the grain ripens, immediately he puts in the sickle, because the harvest has come'" (Mark 4:26–29).

The smallest seed can yield a great thing. We know that a cone the size of an egg can produce a Sequoia tree that is 325 feet tall and weighs 1.6 million pounds. No one could have imagined the spiritual harvest that would arise from the events that occurred on January 1, 1901, on Azusa Street. No one could have imagined how one small anointing of the Holy Spirit on one woman would produce a harvest of over five hundred million!

Let's look at some of the people and events that led up to the Azusa Street Revival.

Charles Fox Parham

Charles Fox Parham (1873–1929) is considered the founder of the modern-day Pentecostal movement. Parham believed that the experience of *glossolalia* (Greek for "tongues," a language never learned) and the power of the Holy Spirit were the mechanisms that would usher in the end-time revival before the coming of the Lord. In 1898 Parham, along with his wife, founded the Bethel Healing Home in Topeka, Kansas. It was a home dedicated to training individuals seeking divine healing.

Parham opened Bethel Bible College in September of 1901. His mission was to train and prepare missionaries for what he believed would be the coming of a mighty outpouring of the Holy Spirit—as evidenced by the baptism of the Holy Spirit with the evidence of speaking in tongues. Although the Bible college lasted only two years, its mission to ignite the modern Pentecostal movement was accomplished.

Agnes N. Ozman

Agnes N. Ozman (1870–1937), like the cone of the giant Sequoia tree, was the seed that was planted to produce the modern day outpouring of the Spirit's baptism. Like so many of us, her passion was to pursue a deeper spiritual walk, which led her to Bethel Bible College. On January 1, 1901, during a "tarrying" (waiting for God to move) service, she spoke in tongues. Ozman did not understand that tongues were the initial evidence of the Spirit's baptism.

She would later write, "Before receiving the Comforter, I did not know that I would speak in tongues when I received the Holy Ghost, for I did not know it was biblical. But after I received the Holy Spirit, speaking in tongues, it was revealed to me that I had the promise of the Father as it is written and as Jesus said ... The next morning, after receiving this mighty gift, I was accosted with questions about my experience of the night before ... I pointed out Bible references to show that I had received the baptism, as Acts 2:4 states: 'And they were all filled with the Holy Ghost and began to speak with other tongues as the Spirit gave them utterance.'"

The following day, and for the next three days, she continued to speak in the language of the Spirit. When she tried to communicate with the other students by writing, she wrote in tongues—whatever that looked like! (*Revival Times Magazine,* London, Volume 3, Issue 1, 2001)

William Joseph Seymour

In 1905 Charles Parham relocated his Bible school in Houston, Texas. William Joseph Seymour (1870–1922) decided that he needed more training and enrolled at Parham's Bible School. Seymour was black, and during this time of racial segregation in the South, he had to sit in a hall where he could only hear the classes through the doorway. Seymour eventually accepted the teaching that speaking in tongues was the initial evidence of the Spirit's baptism.

While still in Houston, he met a woman named Neely Terry, who invited him to Los Angeles to preach at her church. Seymour arrived at the church and began to preach on the baptism with the Holy Spirit with the evidence of speaking in tongues. Don't you love it when someone believes in something even before receiving it?

But as it was in so many other churches and denominations, Seymour was locked out of the building and prevented from any further preaching. I wonder what would have happened if that church had not locked him out? Could *it* have been the place where the modern day explosion would have occurred?

The 214 Bonnie Brae Street Meetings

Edward Lee was a member of the congregation that locked Seymour out of their church. He decided to give Seymour temporary residence at his home. Seymour spent his days in prayer and fasting. Other members of that church began to be led to Seymour's prayer meetings. Lee then invited Seymour to hold his meetings at the home of Richard and Ruth Asberry at 214 Bonnie Brae Street.

The meetings were attended by black women and their husbands. Though the group was small in number, Seymour's commitment to preaching about the Spirit's baptism continued. News of the meetings began to spread to other pastors, and white believers began to attend the meetings, seeking the Spirit's baptism.

On the night of April 9, 1906, Lee asked Seymour to pray for him for a healing. Prior to this, Lee had received a vision from the Lord in which the twelve apostles had come to him and explained speaking in tongues. (No wonder people think Pentecostals are crazy. We *are* crazy—crazy for the things of the Spirit!) Lee asked Seymour to pray for him to receive the Spirit's baptism, and Lee immediately received it and began to speak in tongues as the Spirit gave the utterance. Just as it had happened on the day of Pentecost, something wonderful began, and the results of that moment would reverberate throughout the entire globe. Seymour rushed to the Asberry home and announced what had happened to a packed meeting.

This reminds me of the outpouring that took place in my Bible college in the spring of 1990.

For eighteen months, we had met in the basement of one of the dorms and prayed for the Lord to visit the school in a wonderful way. One morning at about 7:30 a.m., I was visiting with a friend of mine in the dining hall for breakfast. I noticed a table with six students who were laughing and having a wonderful time. Then, suddenly, it became strangely quiet. A lightning bolt came from where the students were and struck me right in the chest. Wow! All of those students were frozen like statues.

Then the Lord spoke to me and told me He had come for a visitation! I ran out of the dining hall and down to one of the classrooms to announce the coming of a visitation. I wondered how I could possibly interrupt their class. When I opened the door, I discovered that the regular teacher wasn't there because she was sick. The substitute was what I call a "Holy Ghost person," meaning that she believed in the stuff. She gave me permission to announce to the class that the Lord was visiting the cafeteria. Then, off I went, back to the cafeteria.

The Lord then directed me to choose a young female student to pray for anyone who came through the archway into the cafeteria. Word got out, and students started coming into the cafeteria. The scene became wild! The girl would walk up to a student, wave her hand over them, and begin to sing in the Spirit. Wham! That student would hit the floor. I began to pray for people, and the whole cafeteria was filled with the glory and presence of the Lord. It is hard to describe the raw power that was in that room. It was frightening!

One student approached me and said she wanted prayer but did not want to fall out under the power. I said okay, her eyes rolled back into her head, and she hit the floor. God pinned her to the floor for over four hours. The only part of her body that she could move was her head. She was under the glory! She asked me why she couldn't move, and I said, "It serves you right for not believing!"

Then I heard the faint sound of worship. The music and the voices were beautiful, almost an out-of-this-world sound. I knew I wanted a tape of that music, so I began to look for the source. The only problem was that there was no source. I investigated every nook and cranny. Then it hit me that I was listening to a heavenly choir. There was an open ladder from the school to the worship center in heaven! I will never forget that moment—the only moment in my life when I experienced the choirs of heaven singing over our meeting. At 12:30 p.m., the meeting ended. What a glorious moment and visitation we had experienced. However, it was not over, as I was soon to discover.

My apartment was ten miles from the school. Late that afternoon, I felt compelled by the Spirit to return to the campus. The campus was located in Barrington, Rhode Island, and was about five miles from the city of Providence, the halfway point between my apartment and the campus. When I got to Providence, the power of the Lord struck my body, and I realized that God was still encamped at the school. I floored it and raced back to the school.

When I got there, I ran to the student snack shop, hoping to walk into something glorious. I walked through the door just in time to see the same girl who had prayed for so many people that morning laying hands on another student, and that student fell out under the power. Then the Holy Ghost told me to pray for anyone coming in.

An hour later, the entire room was filled with students, and my prophetic anointing was on full blast. The dean of students came in and said that this was a true visitation and that we should move to the student hall, the largest of all the rooms at the school.

Students went out and gathered other students. Musicians ran and grabbed their instruments. The worship started, and students began to pray for each other. Some were confessing their sins, and some were rededicating their commitments to the Lord.

Others were worshipping in song. I just sat down and watched the wonderful works of God, and I saw some strange things that night.

One student was prayed for and began to fall forward under the power. His head was headed straight for the corner of the teacher's desk. But before the adrenaline had completely consumed my body, he shifted in midair and hit the floor with no damage.

Another student let out a shriek and jumped almost five feet into the air. I would have loved that anointing for my basketball game!

Two identical twins were participating in a wild scene. They were right next to each other. One was prostrate before the Lord in deep intercession, and her identical sister was right beside her on her back, laughing hysterically in the Holy Ghost, completely drunk on spiritual wine!

Of the entire student body, 75 percent were in that room that night. God had answered our prayers. It was a time to be remembered for a lifetime. The meeting ended at 2:30 a.m. The next morning, there was another visitation in the cafeteria that lasted until lunch. Although this experience only lasted for twenty-four hours, it gave me an understanding of the raw power of a true visitation from God.

Now, let's go back to the scene at Bonnie Brae Street.

When Seymour and Lee entered the Asberry home, Lee began to speak in tongues. Seymour and several others then received the Spirit's baptism and spoke in tongues. One woman, who had received the Spirit's baptism, walked over to the piano and began to play and sing in what sounded like the Hebrew language, thus fulfilling what Paul had said would happen: "And do not be drunk with wine, in which is dissipation; but be filled with the Spirit, speaking to one another in psalms and hymns and *spiritual songs*, singing and making melody in your heart to the Lord" (Ephesians 5:18–19, emphasis added).

The woman at the piano was named was Jennie Moore. She had never played the piano up to that moment, but she would play for the rest of her life and would become the wife of William Seymour. People came from all over to receive and rejoice over this mighty outpouring. The meetings ran all day and into the night. Crowds filled the whole yard as people began to experience the power of the Lord. Eventually, the front porch collapsed, sending many people down the steep front lawn, but no one was hurt. The Asberry home could not handle the great throngs of people, and a larger place was needed. They settled on 312 Azusa Street in Los Angeles.

312 Azusa Street

The building located at 312 Azusa Street was the former home of the Stevens African Methodist Episcopal church. It was a sixty-by-forty-foot, two-story, rectangular building located in a Los Angeles ghetto. Once used as a stable on the first floor, the building was run-down and in need of repair. Like the upper room in Jerusalem, the upper room at Azusa Street became the epicenter for the modern day outpouring of the Spirit's baptism.

There was no fancy lighting, technical gadgetry, or modern sound system. The seating consisted of a few backless chairs holding three redwood planks. The pulpit was a fifteen-cent box where Seymour gave his sermons—and then stuck his head in the box and prayed in the Holy Ghost. There were other rooms where people could be prayed for and receive the Spirit's baptism and healing. As this earthquake of the Spirit's power began to flow in Los Angeles, a physical earthquake was bringing down the city of San Francisco some five hundred miles away.

Humility was the hallmark of these meetings. No one saved seats for top officials or revered ministers. There was no worship warm-up before the meetings to "bring down" the presence of the Lord. No buckets were passed around to collect offerings; there was just a sign in the back stating, "Settle with the Lord." It reminded me of Jesus' humble beginnings in a stable and the camel-hair attire of John the Baptist as he came out of the wilderness to announce the coming of the Messiah.

Meetings ran from ten o'clock in the morning until midnight. Many people came to weep at the altar and to be filled with the wonderful power of the Spirit. Denominational walls fell, as love permeated the meetings. God's power is not reserved for the casual onlooker. In 1 Corinthians 14:1, we are reminded to pursue *agape* love and desire—to have a hot, zealous passion—for spiritual gifts.

So powerful was the presence of the glory of God that people walking outside the building would fall out under the power and receive the Spirit's baptism with the evidence of speaking in tongues! Some people reported a glow coming off the building, and others heard what they thought were explosions and called the fire department. Crowds increased from about three hundred to thousands as visitors poured in from all over the country. Thousands came from around the world, catching the fire and taking it back to their congregations.

The peak of the revival ran from 1906 to 1909. It would be impossible to trace all the spiritual fires that the Azusa Street Revival ignited in the twentieth century. Their meetings are a reminder to all of us of this wonderful gift called the baptism of the Holy Spirit with the evidence of speaking in tongues.

From these meetings came the Pentecostal and charismatic movements throughout the world. I don't like to use the terms *charismatic* or *Pentecostal* to describe the promise and the gift given to us by the Lord in the person and power of the Holy Ghost. When you read the history of these movements, you get lost in all the terminology they used to describe this experience. Denominations then got "marked" as being Pentecostal or charismatic or Spirit-filled. All of these movements were accompanied by scoffers, mockers, and others who totally rejected this experience.

One of the more amazing stories was that of Dennis Bennett. Bennett was appointed to be rector of St. Mark's Episcopal Church in Van Nuys, California in 1953. In 1959 he received the baptism with the Holy Spirit with the evidence of speaking in tongues. Bennett felt obligated to share this experience with his congregation. He decided to share his experience at all three morning services. After the second service, the associate priest resigned. After the third service, Bennett resigned, and a letter was sent out from the church, forbidding anyone else to meet in a church where this doctrine was taught. So much for first-century power. They were not turning down Dennis Bennett; they were turning down Jesus, the Baptizer with the Holy Spirit.

One Sunday morning, my wife and I attended a church in our area. The pastor got up and stated that, because they had been praying for months for revival, when revival came to the city, it would start in their church. I then thought that his church would probably be the last, because the first shall be last and the last shall be first!

On another occasion, I attended a large church in our area. During the worship service, I had a vision. All of a sudden, the walls turned into a tornado of raging fire and began to rotate around this circular sanctuary. At the center top of the room, I could feel the glory of God coming from heaven and penetrating the roof. I braced myself for something spectacular. Then, as the glory began to fall, I heard God say, "Nah, they would just administrate it," and the glory left in a second.

Glory was never meant to be administrated. Begging God to bring "revival" was never the issue in the first century. Real reformation is a reformation of individuals who believe what the early disciples believed. It is one individual receiving the Spirit's power and taking that power whenever and wherever the Spirit guides him or her. Imagine what it would look like if the entire body of Christ had this same faith, power, and purpose!

CONCLUSION

Let your tongue be loosed!

We have learned from Matthew 3:11, Mark 1:8, Luke 3:16, and John 1:33 that Jesus baptizes with the Holy Spirit. We also know that Jesus is our friend. "You are My friends if you do whatever I command you. No longer do I call you servants, for a servant does not know what his master is doing; but I have called you friends, for all things that I heard from My Father I have made known to you" (John 15:14–15).

It is almost unimaginable to think of the Creator and Sustainer of the universe as our friend, but He is! This friend desires to give us everything that pertains to life and the power necessary to live a victorious Christian walk. He commanded His disciples (friends) to tarry in Jerusalem until they were endued with power from on high. He commands us not to leave home without this experience.

People often comment that they are not worthy of the gift of the Spirit's baptism. Somehow, because they have not received it, they think that God is withholding it from them. Let me quench that theology right now.

> Ask, and it will be given to you; seek, and you will find; knock, and it will be opened to you. For *everyone* who asks receives, and he who seeks finds, and to him who knocks it will be opened. Or what man is there among you who, if his son asks for bread, will give him a stone? Or if he asks for a fish, will he give him a serpent? If you then, being evil, know how to give good gifts to your children, how much more will your Father who is in heaven give good things to those who ask Him! (Matthew 7:7–11, emphasis added)

God is withholding nothing from you! He gives much better gifts than we do, and He gives them freely. The Spirit's baptism was for the disciples two thousand years ago, and it is for you today. You are those identified in Acts 2:39 as the ones that are "afar off." All born-again believers have been promised this experience and can receive it, if only they believe. The only hindrance to your Christian walk is unbelief.

We have studied how the traditions of men and rational thinking can quench this experience. The human doctrines of men that attempt to rob Christianity of its spiritual power are at work in the church. I do not like to suggest that some of my brothers in Christ our caught in those doctrines, but they are. We are all subject to spiritual deception without the full understanding of the Word of God.

We have viewed the twentieth-century outpouring of the Azusa Street Revival. We have seen the spread of the Spirit's baptism, which has flooded the globe. Hundreds of millions of Christians have experienced this wonderful gift and promise. Now it is your turn—and it's easy!

Let's make some declarations. Do you know what a spiritual declaration involves? It involves declaring out of your mouth, verbally, what you believe God says in His Word. It is certainly one of the greatest tools or keys to a powerful Christian walk.

"So Jesus answered and said to them, 'Have faith in God. For assuredly, I say to you, *whoever says* to this mountain, "Be removed and be cast into the sea," and does not doubt in his heart, but believes that those things *he says* will be done, he will have whatever *he says*. Therefore I say to you, whatever things *you ask* when you pray, believe that you receive them, and *you will have them*'" (Mark 11:22–24, emphasis added).

A mountain is insurmountable. However, it can be removed when a person has no doubt that it will be removed. When the Holy Spirit told Peter to go to Cornelius' house, He told him to go, "doubting nothing." People must believe what they say in order to receive what they ask for. Jesus, the Baptizer with the Holy Spirit, said that you can have this experience. You can receive it, because it is according to His Word and will. Whatever you say or declare, He backs it up and sets the Holy Spirit in motion. When you asked Christ into your life, you had to receive Him before you saw the fullness of that decision.

Stand before your Father in heaven and declare His Word out loud:

1. "The baptism with the Holy Spirit is for me. I have been promised it, and therefore I will receive it."
2. "The Holy Spirit lives in me. Therefore, any language that has ever been spoken in history, including the language of angels, might come out of my mouth as the Holy Spirit gives the utterance."
3. "I cannot receive this gift by rational thought or by figuring it out. I choose to believe it by faith."

4. "I cannot *think* this experience into existence. My mouth must open, and language must come verbally out of my mouth in the same way that I speak my known language."

Whenever I choose to speak verbally, I have to take a breath and let my language come out. I don't think about it; it just happens automatically. In fact, I don't really remember learning or struggling to speak English. It just came out of my mouth one day. The Holy Spirit will eject this spiritual language out of your mouth as you speak by faith.

So, by faith, without reason, you must allow that spiritual language to come out of your mouth. Don't worry about what you are going to say. Just let those spiritual words flow out of your mouth in Jesus' name!

The Mighty River Flowing Out of Me

There was an old song we used to sing in church. It began like this:

> I have a river of life flowing out of me.
> It makes the lame to walk and the blind to see.
> It opens prison's door and sets the captives free.
> I have a river of life flowing out of me.

Ezekiel 47:1–9 describes a river flowing out of the temple that keeps getting deeper.

> Then he brought me back to the door of the temple; and there was water, flowing from under the threshold of the temple toward the

east, for the front of the temple faced east; the water was flowing from under the right side of the temple, south of the altar. He brought me out by way of the north gate, and led me around on the outside to the outer gateway that faces east; and there was water, running out on the right side.

And when the man went out to the east with the line in his hand, he measured one thousand cubits, and he brought me through the waters; the water came up to my ankles. Again he measured one thousand and brought me through the waters; the water came up to my knees. Again he measured one thousand and brought me through; the water came up to my waist. Again he measured one thousand, and it was a river that I could not cross; for the water was too deep, water in which one must swim, a river that could not be crossed. He said to me, "Son of man, have you seen this?" Then he brought me and returned me to the bank of the river.

When I returned, there, along the bank of the river, were very many trees on one side and the other. Then he said to me: "This water flows toward the eastern region, goes down into the valley, and enters the sea. When it reaches the sea, its waters are healed. And it shall be that every living thing that moves, wherever the rivers go, will live. There will be a very great multitude of fish, because these waters go there; for they will be healed, and everything will live wherever the river goes. (Ezekiel 47:1–9)

It is a river that constantly increases in depth, a river that brings healing and nourishment to the trees on the banks.

Isaiah says this about the rivers: "Do not remember the former things, nor consider the things of old. Behold, I will do a new thing, now it shall spring forth; shall you not know it? I will even make a road in the wilderness and rivers in the desert. The beast of the field will honor Me, the jackals and the ostriches, because I give waters in the wilderness and rivers in the desert, to give drink to My people, My chosen. This people I have formed for Myself; they shall declare My praise" (Isaiah 43:18–21).

I have stood beside the flowing waters of Niagara Falls. There are two things I remember about his experience. First, the water had a constant roar, and second, the water was extremely powerful. From the moment the mighty baptism of the Holy Spirit flowed through my natural body, there has been the constant roar of the powerful rivers of living water flowing out of me.

May you experience this mighty gift and promise!

Made in the USA
Middletown, DE
27 October 2023

41450647R00113